LONDON DOCKS
IN THE 1960S

MARK LEE INMAN

AMBERLEY

Jerry Beckett

A beloved brother-in-law

1956 – 2016

'Nothing can be more stimulating than to watch the ships coming up the Thames – the big ships and the little ships, the battered and the splendid...'

Virginia Woolf – *Selected Essays*

First published 2017

Amberley Publishing
The Hill, Stroud
Gloucestershire, GL5 4EP

www.amberley-books.com

British Library Cataloguing in Publication Data.
A catalogue record for this book is available from the British Library.

ISBN 978 1 4456 6584 9 (print)
ISBN 978 1 4456 6585 6 (ebook)

Typeset in 10pt on 13pt Sabon.
Origination by Amberley Publishing.
Printed in the UK.

Contents

Introduction

I came up to London in October 1965 to read geography at what was then described as Queen Mary College, University of London. The Port of London Authority issued me with a permit to explore and take photographs from the Pool right down to Tilbury. There was one important proviso – that this should only be at weekends. It could be described as heaven. Instead of one ship a week, or two or three at the very most, the wharves were crowded with lines of ships from almost all nations. A 36-exposure film could be used up in one Saturday afternoon!

As an undergraduate I lived in Ilford. It was therefore easy to get the No. 101 from either Manor Park Broadway or Wanstead to the Royal Docks. It was then easy again to walk down the south side of the Albert and back along the north side of the King George V. The West India Docks could be reached by following my usual daily journey to Mile End and then taking a bus to the bottom of Burdett Road. By walking round the West India Docks and coming out of the Millwall docks, the No. 277 could be easily caught back to Mile End. The Surrey Commercial required a trip to what is now Surrey Quays, while Tilbury was easily reached by train from Barking.

After graduation I continued to live in Ilford, so it remained possible to continue my Saturday adventures to the Royal and the West India Docks, and so some post-1968 photographs appear. However, most of the pictures were taken in the Royal Docks, with a few excursions to the West India and even fewer down to Tilbury and the Surrey Commercial Docks.

It was a time of considerable variety. In 1965 it was still possible to see Union-Castle and British India passenger liners in the Royal Docks. Some of the cargo liners also carried up to twelve passengers – the maximum allowed before it was necessary to provide medical facilities. There were survivors from the pre-war era. Veteran Liberty, Victory and Empire standard cargo vessels, along with US-owned C2 types from the war years, still appeared. The only obvious changes were that the newer ships were usually slightly bigger and faster.

Some ships had quite eventful careers, while others went about their lawful occasions well out of the limelight. As a result, the length of caption and amount of detail will vary enormously.

Another feature was that many shipping companies using the London docks at that time had large fleets. As a result, some companies will be well represented. In these cases, a little about the history of the company is provided.

The container revolution, still only on the horizon in the early-to-mid 1960s, did not happen overnight. Many of the ports that traditional ships served were much slower to adapt to container handling. The revolution demanded major changes in both ships and harbour facilities. As a result, many of the ships depicted survived with their original owners well into the late 1970s and beyond. Others eked out a less glamorous life under dubious foreign flags.

There is a walkway by the Thames from Tower Bridge along the south bank to the Thames Barrier and along the north bank to Island Gardens. The book will follow that route from Tower Bridge, through the Surrey Commercial Docks and the West India Docks and thence to the Royal Docks and finally to Tilbury.

It is gratifying to record that, despite the momentous changes and the disappearance of the traditional dock areas, a modern-day walk along the Thames, such as upstream from Tilbury Fort towards Tilbury Docks or downstream towards the Gateway, still reveals a busy river with substantial amounts of tonnage plying its trade.

In researching histories I have had to dig out my old Ian Allen ship-spotting books. Two editions of Bert Moody's *Ocean Ships* have proved an essential source of initial information. Mitchell and Sawyer's excellent *Empire Ships of World War II, Oceans, the Forts and the Parks* and *The Liberty Ships* are three excellent tomes that have proved invaluable. In addition, Andrew Wiltshire's *Looking Back at Traditional Cargo Ships*, Ambrose Greenaway's *Cargo Liners* and Moss and Hume's *Shipbuilders to the World* have filled in vital details. For specific shipping companies, H. M. Le Fleming's *Ships of the Holland America Line*, C. H. Milsom's *Blue Funnel: The Later Years*, Laurence Dunn's *Ships of the Union-Castle Line* and William H. Miller's *British India Steam Navigation Co. Liners* admirably filled in other forgotten details. Obviously, in this age of high technology, acknowledgement and gratitude must be offered to the many historic ship, ship-spotting, shipping company and shipyard websites. Even so, any mistakes or misinterpretations I have to take full responsibility for.

The Pool and Tower Bridge

Monte Amboto, built 1929, 2,955 tons. Aznar, Spain.
Built in Bilbao. This was a lucky shot while having a summer Saturday wander around London in 1966. Perhaps she is the oldest ship in the collection. Not present in either of my Moody *Ocean Ships* books, she was very near to the end of her days.

Torres de Cuarto. Spanish.
Not much is known about this ship – however, it is the background that is most interesting. The cranes and New Fresh Wharf Limited have gone, with new buildings on the site instead. The building on the extreme left remains but what is also of interest is the parapet of the old Rennie-designed London Bridge of 1831. Its sale to the United States and subsequent delivery to Arizona were then two years in the future.

Baltic Sun, built 1962, 3,505 tons. United Baltic.

Originally United Baltic was formed in 1919 as a joint venture between Andrew Weir's Bank Line and the Danish East Asiatic Co. Early traffic was a feeder service for Baltic immigrants into London to enable a connection with emigrant liners to North America. The operation moved to Hays Wharf in 1922. This was a service jointly operated to the Baltic with Polish Ocean Lines. The ship herself was sold to Singapore in 1973. However, it is again the background that is of interest. The cranes and buildings of the historic Hay's Wharf have disappeared, to be replaced by the ultra-modern monstrosity that is City Hall. Other more pleasing developments have appeared or are appearing along both sides of Tower Bridge Road, leaving Tower Bridge as the only constant factor in this view.

Andrew Weir took 100 per cent control of United Baltic in 1982 and the company was still operational in 2002.

Surrey Commercial

The Surrey Commercial docks date back to the early seventeenth century. The Rotherhithe peninsula was deemed unsuitable for farming, but proximity to the river made it an ideal potential dock area. In 1620 the Pilgrim Fathers' ship *Mayflower* loaded before setting sail to Southampton and the long transatlantic voyage to religious freedom. The Howland Great Wet Dock (named for the landowner) was dug out in 1696. Eighteenth-century whaling led to its renaming to the Greenland Dock, while in the nineteenth century traffic from Scandinavia and the Baltic led to considerable expansion. Eventually 85 per cent of the peninsula, some 460 acres, was taken up with a dock system consisting of nine docks, six timber ponds and a canal.

The docks suffered considerable damage during the Second World War. Post war, the docks were unable to accommodate larger ships and neither did they lend themselves to conversion for containerisation. They were closed in 1969 and eventually, after years of dereliction, redeveloped in the late 1980s and 1990s.

La Selva, built 1958, 7,014 tons. Buries Markes Ltd.
Built in Valencia, Spain, she was sold in 1967 and again in 1981. After periods of lay-up, she was eventually sold for breaking up in 1984 and scrapped at Gadani Beach in India.
 Buries Markes finally got out of shipping in 1990.

Salechard, built 1965, 2,987 tons. USSR.
When this picture was taken during the summer of 1966, the vessel was only a year old. In 1989 she was renamed *Uniforce* under the flag of St Vincent. On 1 March 1993, while en route from Mukkala to Port Soudan, she suffered a major engine-room fire. Abandoned, she ran aground between Mukalla and Aden. She was refloated on 5 March and broken up at Gadani Beach in July that year.

Svirvles, built 1965, 4,896 tons. USSR. Surrey Commercial.
Built in the Zhdanov yard in what was then Leningrad, she appears to be just another Soviet timber ship in the Surrey Commercial docks, summer 1966. However, this ship was destined for a more glamorous future. Despite being only two years old, in 1967 she was converted into a space control and monitoring ship, and renamed *Borovichi*. She was eventually broken up at Alang in November 1990.

Andalusian, built 1950, 3,913 tons. Ellerman. Surrey Commercial.
The Ellerman Line was a large group with a worldwide network of trading routes. Not all the Ellerman Line ships were named for cities. Honouring a delightful part of Spain, this was a difficult shot in the Surrey Commercial docks in the summer of 1966. The ship was very near the end of her days with Ellerman.

    Those interested in the technical aspects of photography will be impressed by the quality of my Color-Skopar lens, which makes the rope very sharp and the ensign and name details very clear, despite being at the edge of the photograph.

Djajadwitja (ex-*River Burdekin*), built 1943. Indonesia. Surrey Commercial.
As I suspected, a wartime-built ship, but not the easiest to research. She was built by Evans Deakin, Brisbane, for the Australian government. After the war, she became part of the Australian National Line fleet. She was then sold to Indonesia in 1959 and renamed *Djajadwitja*. After several Indonesian owners, she was scrapped at Kaohsiung in 1971.

Spyros Polemis. Greece. Surrey Commercial.
Considering the limitations of the Surrey Commercial docks, this was quite a large ship. She was named for a celebrity in the Greek shipping industry.

Rimja Dan, built 1960, 3,407 tons. Lauritzen, Denmark. Surrey Commercial.
Built in Germany, she was sold in 1968 but retained Scandinavian ownership and flag until 1974. She was sold on further in 1974 and again in 1978, before foundering (so the website tactfully describes it!) in April 1983.

Due their longstanding polar associations, particularly supporting Antarctic exploration, Lauritzen Line ships have distinctive red hulls for ease of observation. Laurtizen Line still operates, specialising in bulk dry cargo and liquid gas transport, and retains the distinctive red hulls.

Podolv. USSR. Surrey Commercial.
I hope my transliteration is correct; most ships where the national alphabet is different usually have some readily visible transliteration. However, in this case, there was none that was readily and easily visible.

One of a large class of colliers built in Poland during 1952–1960 for the USSR, she is seen unloading (but not coal!) in the Surrey Commercial docks in the summer of 1966.

Baltic Venture, 1965. 1,581 tons. United Baltic Corporation. Surrey Commercial.
Built by Doxfords of Sunderland, she was lengthened by Swan Hunter in 1970. She was sold to Cyprus in 1981 and then again to ownership in the Maldive Islands in 1985.

   Following a major fire in March 1988, she was broken up at Valinokkam, Tamil Nadu, India, the following October.

West India Docks

The West India Docks is series of three docks established on the Isle of Dogs and first opened in 1802. They owed their origin to one Robert Lilligan (1746–1809), a wealthy, successful West Indian merchant and shipowner. He was appalled by the level of theft and delay at the riverside wharves, and so he promoted the development of a wet dock surrounded by a high wall. The West India Dock Act of 1799 was the first Act of Parliament to promote a dock. The first two northern docks were opened in 1802. The third (South) dock was added in 1860, replacing an unprofitable canal originally built by the City of London Corporation. The West India Docks were taken over by the Port of London Authority in 1909.

   From 1960 to 1980, trade declined dramatically to almost nothing. The docks were unsuited to container traffic and much of the traditional, locally generated export trade had disappeared. The docks were closed in 1980.

The Canary Wharf development reduced the size of the docks; the Jubilee Line station at Canary Wharf was actually constructed within the middle dock and subsequent developments, such as the new Crossrail station, have taken place within the former north dock.

However, the docks remain open for ships, and certain structural features such as walls are protected by national and government policy. The former south dock is still used regularly by visiting military vessels, since it is the furthest point upstream where they can still be turned round.

The Museum of the London Docklands occupies part of the original dock building.

Ben Line

Bencleuch, built 1949, 7,863 tons. Ben.
Built by Scotstoun, she was scrapped in 1972. The original company dated from 1839, when it was W. & A. Thomson. The company became involved in trading to the Far East in 1859. It took the name Ben Line Steamers in 1919. In 1966 the company combined with other operators to form Associated Container Transport, providing a container service from European ports to the Far East, Australia and New Zealand. Although it acquired Sheaf Shipping of Newcastle in 1976, in 1991 it combined with the Danish East Asiatic Line to operate a weekly service to the Far East. However, the remaining ship was sold in 1992.

From the very beginning, the ships were named for Scottish 'bens', meaning mountains, from the Gaelic word for head or top.

Opposite above: Benlawers, built 1970, 12,784 tons. Ben Line. West India.
Despite the Ben-Ellerman container venture being formed in 1968, the conventional *Benlawers* was delivered from the nationalised Upper Clyde Shipbuilders in 1970. After only eight years she was sold to Singapore to become the *Globe Express* and again to Italian buyers in 1981 becoming the *Uniceb*. Converted to a livestock carrier, in 1996 while en route from Fremantle to Aqaba she suffered a major engine room fire and sank east of the Seychelles. Some 67,000 sheep were lost in the disaster.

Bencruachan, built 1968, 12,094 tons. Ben.

Again, bigger and possibly faster but already out of date. However, she had been modified to carry a few containers. As such she came close to becoming what the Germans were calling an 'Omni-ship'. Even so, she has been described as the *Cutty Sark* of her age, fast, elegant but sadly already out of date. Unlike her sisters, she remained with Ben Line until scrapped in Kaohsiung in 1980.

My late father-in-law, a great lover of the Scottish Highlands and particularly the area around Loch Awe, always referred to both mountain and ship as 'Ben crew cut!'

Benedin (ex-*City of Winnipeg*), built 1956, 7,716 tons. Ben.
Built originally for the Ellerman Line, she was sold to Ben Line in 1968 before returning to Ellerman Line in 1972 as the *City of Delhi*. She was sold in 1976 and eventually broken up at Chittagong in 1988.

For the purist and ardent nationalist, this was a hybrid name – there is no Benedin! It is a corruption of 'Edin', as in Dunedin or Edinburgh.

Benledi, built 1965, 11,898 tons. Ben.
One of a quartet of fast (21 knots) cargo liners built at Connell's yard in Scotstoun. She was sold to Italy in 1972 to become the *Da Noli* and on to Panamanian interests in 1980, before being laid up in Greece in 1982. She was wrecked during a cyclone in the Bay of Bengal while en route for scrapping in August 1987.

Benwyvis, built 1966, 11,959 tons. Ben.
The second of the Benledi quartet, she was sold to Italy in 1972 to become the *Da Recco* and scrapped at La Spezia following a fire in 1979.

Benvalla, built 1962, 11,931 tons. Ben.
One of the Connell-built 'Benloyal' class of ships, differing from the pioneering *Benloyal* by being diesel driven. The ships were capable of 20 knots and designed to provide a new fast service from Europe to the Far East. Following the containerisation of the Far East services in 1972, the *Benvalla* was sold to Chinese buyers to become the *Yichun* and later the *Hua Chun*. She was broken up in China in 1992.

Harrison Line

Inventor, built 1964, 9,171 tons. Harrison Line.

Dating from 1853, the Liverpool-based Harrison line originally traded imported brandy from France. Later they were involved in trading with Spain, Portugal and the Mediterranean. They were also involved in shipping brandy from Liverpool to Demerara. The company became part of the West Indian Shipping Conference in 1904.

In 1970 the company diversified into bulk carriers and joined a Caribbean container consortium in 1976. The Harrison Line ceased to exist when the last of the liner trades were transferred to P&O Nedlloyd.

They named their ships after 'trades and professions', a term that was widely interpreted. The *Inventor*, depicted here, was the fourth ship to carry the name. She was eventually sold to Singaporean interests in 1981.

Explorer, built 1961, 7,200 tons. Harrison Line.

The Harrison Line also operated from London, the West Indies and Guyana. This was the fourth ship to carry the name. She was sold to Greece in 1979.

Trader, built 1966, 6,488 tons. Harrison Line.
At well under 10,000 tons gross, just over 400 feet in length and with a service speed of only 16 knots, the *Trader* rather bucked the trend for bigger and faster. She was sold in 1980 to Singaporean interests to become the *Bangpa-In*.

Woodwren (ex-*Eddystone*), built 1954, 968 tons. Harrison Line General Steam Navigation.
General Steam had been operating along the Thames and the North Sea and Channel ports since 1924. The company was eventually absorbed into the P&O Group. *Woodwren* was sold to Yugoslavia in 1969.

Ravenfjell, built 1955, 1,937 tons. Harrison Line Olsen & Ugelstad, Norway.
She operated between Europe and the Great Lakes initially, in the days before the St Lawrence
Seaway – hence her rather stubby look to enable her to negotiate the locks.

Prins Alexander, built 1947, 2,322 tons. Harrison Line Fjell-Oranje Line, Netherlands.
The Great Lakes service was jointly operated by the Norwegian Olsen & Ugelstad and the Dutch
Oranje Line. Established in 1956, it was jointly marketed as Fjell-Oranje Line.

Dorothea Bolten, built 1970, 4,935 tons. Harrison Line Germany.
Surprisingly, traditional tramp steamers were still being built as late as 1970. Built in Lubeck, she was sold in 1978 to become the *Bachie*, then again in 1981 to become the *Terenga* and in 1986 to become the *Beryte*. She was eventually scrapped in 2002.

West India Miscellany

Bonanza, built 1953, 7,148 tons. Fred Olsen, Norway.
The distinctive and clearly visible feature of this ship is her impressive figurehead. Reminiscent of the old days of sailing ships, Fred Olsen ships carried these until the 1960s.

Nebraska, built 1966, 4,505 tons. DFDS, Denmark.
The first of eight ships delivered to DFDS to boost their trading with both the United States and Latin America. Competition from the new container and ro-ro ships caused this venture to cease in 1967, and the ships were transferred to running to the US Gulf states. In 1972, the *Nebraska* was sold to become the Italian *D'Azeglio* and was scrapped at La Spezia in 1985.

DFDS always obligingly painted the ship's name in large letters on the side of the hull. DFDS ships and containers can still be seen on a regular basis today.

Ohio, built 1956, 2,812 tons. DFDS, Denmark. Royal Albert.
As above.

Afram River, built 1962, 5,321 tons. Black Star Line, Ghana.
Built by Helsingor Vaerft, Helsingor, she was sold to Greece in 1971 and sold again in 1976 to become the Stavronikita, still under the Greek flag. While en route from Ireland to Barbados she caught fire. Rendered useless, she was laid up until purchased in 1978 by the Barbadian government and scuttled to form an artificial reef.

Kulpawn River, built 1962, 5,001 tons. Black Star Line, Ghana.
Another of the eight new-build ships for Black Star Line, also built in the Netherlands. She was sold for scrapping in 1980.

Cluj, built 1962, 3,090 tons. Romania.
Small Romanian cargo ship unloading in the summer of 1966.

Ariosto, built 1946, 2,195 tons. Ellerman Wilson Line.
Ellerman Lines acquired the Wilson Line, which operated short sea services out of Hull in 1916. It became Ellerman Wilson a year later, but never took the Ellerman Lines corporate identity. The *Ariosto* is seen arriving at the West India Docks in the summer of 1966. She was scrapped a year later. All the Ellerman Wilson services, except those in the North Sea, were eventually absorbed into Ellerman City Lines, with the remaining ships sold in 1978.

Catanian, built 1958, 1,408 tons. Ellerman Line.
Not all Ellerman Line ships had 'city' names. Built by Henry Robb of Leith, the *Catanian* was sold to the Maldives in 1972 and renamed *Ocean Glory*. It was sold for scrapping in 1987.

Famor (ex-*Benjamin R. Milam*), built 1943, 7,176 tons. Uruguay.
Built as part of the Liberty ship programme by the Todd Houston Shipbuilding Corporation at Irish Bend Island, Houston (TX), she was completed in June 1943. Following a boiler room explosion and her subsequent sinking at Locust Point, Baltimore, in March 1945, she was raised, repaired and sold off commercially in 1947. She became the *Famor* in 1964 and was scrapped at Santander in October 1968. Not a bad lifespan for a class of ship described in a US Congressional report as a 'five-year ship'.

S. A. Pioneer (ex-*Sira*), built 1952, 9,684. Safmarine, South Africa.
Built in Glasgow for Norwegian owners as the *Sira,* she was purchased by Safmarine in 1957 and
scrapped in 1972 following a collision.

Havkatt, built 1959, 10,365 tons. Norway.
Described as a bulker, and built between 1950 and 1960. She was sold in 1969 to become the
Daphinis and again in 1975 to become the *Rasamala.*

La Heve, built 1947, 4,310 tons. CGT (the French Line), France.
CGT was both France's equivalent to and a serious rival of Cunard during the interwar period. Like Cunard, they also operated cargo liners. As part of the post-war rebuilding programme, the *La Heve* was one of a class of ships built for the Caribbean service. *La Heve* was built by Harland & Wolff but in their Govan (Glasgow) yard. Not long after this photograph was taken, she was sold to South American interests, before eventually being scrapped at the end of the 1970s.

Guadeloupe (ex-*Canteleu*), built 1949, 4,294 tons. CGT, France.
Although broadly similar to CGT's own La Hague class, she was acquired from Cie France Nav. in 1953 and sold to Saudi Arabia in 1972 to become the *Asir*.

La Coubre, built 1948, 4,310 tons. CGT, France.
Part of CGT's post-war rebuilding programme for the Caribbean services, she was involved in a major explosion while unloading explosives in Havana, Cuba, in March 1960. Despite being badly damaged, she was towed into dry dock in Havana and repaired. She returned to service and remained with CGT until 1972, when she was sold to Cyprus and renamed *Barbara*.

Avis Ornis, (ex-*New York City*), built 1956, 5,603 tons. Gibraltar.
Built originally by Redhead's in South Shields as the Bristol City Line *New York City*, she came under the Gibraltarian flag in 1968. Photographed not long after the change of ownership, she still sports the Bristol City Line star on her bow. She was later sold to Cypriot interests and eventually on to Chinese ownership.

The Royal Group of Docks

The three docks that make up this group were completed between 1855 and 1921 on former riverside marshes on a long meander of the River Thames in what is now the London Borough of Newham. The Victoria and Albert docks were constructed by the London & St Katherine Docks Co. to provide berths for ships that could not be accommodated further upstream. The docks were a great commercial success, becoming London's principal docks during the first half of the twentieth century. They specialised in the import and unloading of foodstuffs, with rows of granaries and refrigerated warehouses being sited along the quays. The combination of size and the additional provision of finger quays gave them a collective span of over 12 miles of quaysides, providing a maximum capacity of berthing space for just over 100 ships.

The first dock to be completed was the Royal Victoria in 1855, followed by the Royal Albert in 1880. The latter gave access to Gallions Reach, effectively creating a dock area that ran from the east to the west of the area. This development led to the rival

Jamaica Planter, built 1959, 6,159 tons. Jamaica Banana Producer Steamship, Jamaica.
Bananas were one of the many cargoes shipped into the Royal docks. The *Jamaica Planter* was one of my first photographs in the autumn of 1965. Built on the Clyde in 1959, she was sold to Singapore to become the *Fine Fruit* and scrapped in Taiwan in 1976.

East & West India Docks Co. to develop Tilbury Docks even further downstream. The ruinous competition led to the establishment of the Port of London Authority in 1909. The King George V dock was opened in 1921 and the PLA reserved land for a fourth dock to the north of the Royal Albert, but this never materialised. The three docks formed the largest enclosed docks in the world, with a water area of 250 acres and an overall estate of 1,100 acres. Putting such figures in perspective, that is the equivalent of the whole of central London from Hyde Park to Tower Bridge.

Although the docks recovered from the wartime ravages, decline set in during the 1960s as there was progressive moving towards containerisation. Even so, the docks survived until closure to commercial traffic in 1981.

Even so, it is still an area that encourages exploration. The London Capital Ring walkway emerges onto the former north quay of the Royal Albert dock by the University of East London campus. It provides splendid, if noisy, views of London City Airport, which occupies the former south quay of the Royal Albert and the north quay of the King George V dock. The walker is directed along the former quay, while the bridge between the Royal Albert dock and the dock basin now honours the Olympic rower Sir Steve Redgrave. The walk then heads for the river, with walkers following the river across both sets of former dock gates to reach North Woolwich.

La Laguna, built 1960, 9,306 tons. Buries Markes Ltd. Royal Albert.
Sold and re-registered under the Liberian flag. After several changes of name, ownership and flag, she was scrapped in 1985.

Hornby Grange, built 1946, 10,785 tons. Houlder Bros. Royal Albert (Albert Basin).
The Houlder Line operated between London and the River Plate. From 1914 it was jointly involved with Furness Withy. Many of the ships carried the distinctive 'Grange' name suffix.

Built by Hawthorn Leslie at Hebburn-on-Tyne, she was the last of four war-built ships that were specially designed meat carriers. When delivered in 1946 she had the distinction of being the largest chilled-meat carrier in the world. She eventually finished her days in 1972 with the Royal Mail Line as the *Douro.*

Royston Grange, built 1959, 10,262 tons. Houlder Bros. Royal Albert.
It seems that my enthusiasm was not dampened by the weather. Built by Hawthorn Leslie, on 12 May 1972 while en route from Buenos Aires to London she was sadly lost with all hands as the result of a collision with a Liberian tanker in the Punta Indico Channel of the River Plate, some 35 miles off Montevideo. The tragic loss of life was caused by the fire from the tanker's cargo and the *Royston Grange*'s own cargo of butter. The accident happened at night, when most of the passengers and crew were asleep.

The Houlder Line ceased operations in 1985.

United Netherlands

The company was formed after the First World War. Dutch shipping companies saw a gap in the market because German companies had disappeared and demand was high. The directors of several existing Dutch shipping companies decided to establish a new company to fill the gap. The most notable gap was from Europe to East Africa, formerly operated by Deutsche Ost Afrika Linie. In addition it was offering competition to the British Union-Castle Line and British India Line. Operations were expanded to serve India by taking over services operated by Holland America Line (NASM), to Australia by taking over Rotterdam Lloyd operations and, later, to West Africa. Services to South Africa were reinforced by the acquisition of the newly formed and, initially, government-supported Holland South Africa Line (NZASM). The early fleet comprised of many ships acquired under wartime reparations.

As such it became the Netherlands equivalent of Union-Castle, the P&O British India Group and, to some extent, with its links to the Netherlands East Indies, Alfred Holt's Blue Funnel Line.

Gaasterkerk (ex-*Reed Victory*), built 1945, 7,637 tons. United Netherlands (VNSMNV), Netherlands. Royal Albert.
An unusual shot, as ships berthed in the Royal docks usually faced upstream. The Victory ship was a development of the earlier wartime Liberty ship. They were slightly larger and had more powerful engines. Some of the earlier design problems and welding problems encountered with the Liberty ships were also corrected. Laid down by the Oregon Shipbuilding Corporation at Portland, Oregon, on 20 February 1945, she was delivered on 29 April, a mere sixty-seven days later. Sold to VNSMNV in 1946, she was scrapped in Whampoa in 1970 after twenty-four years of service.

In the post-Second World War era, passenger traffic declined because of political troubles and competition from airlines. To tackle the container revolution, the company merged with Royal Rotterdam Lloyd (KRL) and other Dutch shipping companies in 1969. This eventually became the Koninklijke Nedlloyd Group, and eventually P&O Nedlloyd Container Line, now part of the Maersk Group.

Grootekerk (ex-*Gonzaga Victory*), built 1945, 7,647 tons. United Netherlands (VNSMNV). Royal Albert.
The 688th Victory ship to be built, she was also laid down in the yard Oregon Shipbuilding Corporation in April 1945 and delivered the following June – seventy-three days later. She was acquired by VNSMNV in 1946. She was scrapped at Whampoa in 1970.
Twenty years after the cessation of hostilities, to capture two Victory ships still operated by the same company was quite an achievement.

Heemskerk, built 1949, 6,293 tons. VNSMNV, the Netherlands. Royal Albert.
Originally built by Nederland Dockyard in Amsterdam as the *Aagtekerk*, she was sold in 1969 to Italian buyers, becoming the *Albertoemme,* and was scrapped at La Spezia in 1978.

Laarderkerk, built 1958, 8,919 tons. VNSMNV, the Netherlands. Royal Albert.
Built by Howaldtswerke in Hamburg, she was transferred to Nedlloyd in 1970. In 1977 she was sold to Panamanian interests to become the *Sea Cloud* and was scrapped at Kaohsiung in 1979.

Ouwerkerk, built 1954, 7,148 tons. VNSMNV, the Netherlands.
A misty rather than foggy day in London town. This photograph also shows the problem of barges obscuring good pictures of ships.
　　Built by Nederland Dockyard in Amsterdam, she was also transferred to Nedlloyd in 1970. In 1973 she was sold to Indonesian buyers and renamed the *Gemilang*. She was scrapped at Belawan, Sumatra, Indonesia, in 1982.

Blue Star Line

Blue Star Line owed its origins to the enterprising, Liverpool-based Vestey brothers. They were importing frozen meat from South America. The high shipping charges prompted the operation of their own ships from 1911. After the First World War, the 'star' names appeared and, as the operations expanded, the company was regarded as serious competition to the Royal Mail group. In the post-war era, the company developed global interests and became one of the founding partners of Associated Container Transport. Blue Star was bought by P&O Nedlloyd in 1998 and the last truly Blue Star liner was broken up in 2003.

The Blue Star Line was not entirely remote from the High Street. Also part of the Vestey empire was Dewhurst, the butchers.

Fremantle Star, built 1960, 8,403 tons. Blue Star. Royal Albert.
Blue Star Line ships were always among some of the most elegant and stylish of ships. Built by Cammell Laird at Birkenhead, she served briefly with the Lamport & Holt Line in 1965. She was sold in 1979 to become the *Catarina* under the Singaporean flag, but was then broken up the same year in Kaohsiung.

Iberia Star (ex-*Anselm*, ex-*Baudounville*), built 1954, 10,854 tons. Blue Star Line. Royal Albert. Built by Cockerill, Belgium, as the *Baudounville*, she was sold in 1961 to the Liverpool-based Booth Line to become the *Anselm*. In 1963 she was transferred to the Blue Star Line to become the *Iberia Star*. In October 1965 she became the *Australasia*, before being reregistered in Singapore in 1970 and eventually broken up in Taiwan in 1973.

This photograph, one of my first in the Royal Docks, was taken prior to her being dry docked during the change from *Iberia Star* to *Australasia*.

She is pictured here as the *Australasia*.

Rhodesia Star (ex-*Premier*, ex-*Estero*), built 1943, 8,467 tons. Blue Star Line. Royal Victoria.
Not one of my better pictures. However, she had had an interesting history. One of nineteen escort aircraft carriers built originally as class C3 merchant ships but completed as carriers at the Seattle-Tacoma yard in Tacoma (Wash). She was then converted by Burrard Dockyard to Royal Navy specification and commissioned as HMS *Premier* in January 1944. She became the *Rhodesia Star* in 1948 and was sold to Bahamian interests in 1967. This photograph must have been taken almost at the end of her time with Blue Star.

The *Rhodesia Star* had previously visited Swansea, possibly around 1961/2. I went on board and recall the somewhat jaundiced chief officer expressing a very pessimistic view of the future to us teenagers who might have felt the call of the sea. He saw a future of bigger ships, fewer ships and much smaller crews. The prophecy very quickly became a true and harsh reality.

Auckland Star, built 1958, 11,799 tons. Blue Star. Royal Albert.
She was built by Cammell Laird in Birkenhead, initially for the Bermudan subsidiary Salient Shipping. She was sold for breaking-up in India in 1978.

Tasmania Star, built 1950, 12,605 tons. Blue Star. Royal Albert.
A sister ship to the *Auckland Star,* this vessel was also built by Cammell Laird, albeit eight years earlier. At the time she was regarded as one of the largest and fastest (17 knots) cargo liners in service. She was equipped with 572,000 cubic feet of refrigerated space and a 60-ton derrick to enable heavy cargo forward of the superstructure. She was sold in 1975 and scrapped in Kaohsiung.

Canberra Star, built 1956, 8,398 tons. Blue Star Line.
She was the first of five sisters built on a fixed-price contract with penalties for late delivery by Bremer Vulkan in Germany. The decision caused considerable controversy at the time. Renamed *Buenos Aires Star* in 1972 to replace the former *Hobart Star* for the South American run, she was sold for scrapping in 1979.

Dunedin Star, built 1950, 7,344 tons. Blue Star Line.
Originally built by Alexander Stephen at Linthouse on the Clyde for the Lancashire Shipping Co. as the *Bolton Castle* for trade with China. The revolution substantially reduced this trade, so she was sold on the stocks to Blue Star Line. Smaller than many of the Blue Star Line ships and with only limited refrigerated capacity, she nevertheless served the Blue Star Group for twenty-five years. In 1968, she was transferred to Lamport & Holt Line as the *Roland* and plied the South America trade until sold in 1975 to Cypriot buyers. After two more changes of ownership, she was eventually scrapped at Gadani Beach in 1978.

California Star (ex-*Empire Clarendon*), built 1945, 7,930 tons. Blue Star Line. Royal Victoria.
Built by Harland & Wolff as part of a programme for fast (14 knots) standard cargo ships upgraded with refrigerated cargo capacity. She had between 420,000 and 450,000 cubic feet of refrigerated capacity. She was a 'sister' to the NZ liner *Rakaia* (ex-*Empire Abercorn*) and similar in specification to the *Port Hobart* (ex-*Empire Wessex*). She was scrapped in 1969.

Above: *English Star*, built 1950, 10,174 tons. Blue Star Line. Royal Victoria.
Built by Fairfields, Glasgow, to replace tonnage lost during the war. She was sold for scrapping in Kaohsiung in 1973.

Opposite above: *Gladstone Star*, built 1957, 10,725 tons. Blue Star Line. Royal Victoria.
Again, this is not one of the most flattering pictures, due to the practicalities of photography in the Royal Victoria dock. However, it does show the cruiser spoon stern that was favoured by Blue Star Line. This was another of the German Bremer Vulkan-built ships, initially for the Bermuda subsidiary Salient Shipping. She was sold to Maltese interests in 1982 and scrapped at Gadani Beach.

Opposite below: *Rockhampton Star*, built 1958, 10,619 tons. Blue Star. Royal Albert.
She was built by Cammell Laird. She was sold to Panamanian interests in 1981 but was sold again in 1982 for breaking up in Karachi. In 1983 she was sold on to Bengali ship-breakers and arrived in Chittagong on 20 June.

Scottish Star, built 1950, 10,174 tons. Blue Star. King George V Dock.
A sister ship to the *English Star* and also built by Fairfields. This photograph illustrates the unhappy aspect of the summer of 1966 – the seaman's strike. The ship appears to be laid up alongside a Union-Castle liner in the King George V dock. The following year she was caught in the Suez Canal closure and declared a constructive total loss in 1969. Towed out of the canal in 1975, she was sold to Greek interests, complete with her cargo. Towed to Piraeus to be unloaded, she was laid up until sold to Spanish breakers in 1979 in a typically ignominious ending to a ship that had spent over 40 per cent of her operational life out of service.

Townsville Star, built 1957, 10,725 tons. Blue Star Line. Royal Albert.
Captured in the dry dock facility that was situated at the west end of the Royal Albert dock. She was built by Bremer Vulkan in Germany and, for part of her operational life, she flew the Bermudan flag. In 1980 she was trapped for two months by the Iran-Iraq war at Khorramshahr and was eventually scrapped at Kaohsiung soon after.

Glen Line

The Glen Line owed its origins to a Glasgow-based partnership founded in the mid-nineteenth century – hence the 'Glen' names. Taken over by the Royal Mail Group in 1910, it was integrated with the Shire Line – hence some ships were named for Scottish glens and others for Welsh shires. The collapse of the Royal Mail Group in 1930 eventually led in 1935 to its acquisition and rescue by rival Liverpool-based Alfred Holt's Blue Funnel Line, becoming Holt's London operation. Ships were frequently transferred between the two fleets by merely changing the name and painting the funnel in the appropriate colour.

Cardiganshire (ex-*Bellerophon*), built 1950, 7,724 tons. Glen Line. Royal Albert.
The *Cardiganshire* had started life with Blue Funnel as the Robb Caledon-built *Bellerophon*, transferring to the Glen Line in October 1957. She returned to Blue Funnel in 1972, reverting to her original name before being passed to the Elder Dempster line in 1975. Sold in 1976 to Saudi interests and becoming the *Obhor*, she was eventually broken up at Gadani Beach in Pakistan in 1978.

Glenroy, built 1938, 8,959 tons. Glen Line.

One of eight twin-screw fast (18 knots) cargo liners ordered by Blue Funnel for the Glen Line. They were to form the unmistakable standard Blue Funnel/Glen Line profile for the next twenty-five years. For quick delivery of all the ships, four yards were employed to do the building. The *Glenroy* was built by Robb Caledon, Dundee, and she was requisitioned by the Admiralty in October 1939. She served first as a fast transport before conversion to an LSI in June 1940. She was returned to the Glen Line in 1946 and scrapped around 1966.

Glenbeg (ex-*Diomed*), built 1956, 7,984 tons. Glen Line. Royal Victoria.

The next three Glen Line ships illustrate how transfers were made between Blue Funnel and the Glen Line. The *Glenbeg* was built by Robb Caledon, Dundee, as the Blue Funnel *Diomed*; she was transferred to the Glen Line in 1970. Returned to Blue Funnel and reverting to her original name in 1972, she was sold in 1973 to Macau interests, albeit flying the Somali flag. She was eventually scrapped at Kaohsiung in 1983.

This is an unusual picture in that most ships berthed in the Royal docks faced west – upstream.

Glenfruin (ex-*Dolius*), built 1956, 7,964 tons. Glen. King George V Dock.
Built by Harland & Wolff, she was transferred from Blue Funnel in 1970, transferred back in 1972, and then sold to Macau interests, but flying the Somali flag. In 1977 she was sold to the Chinese Bureau of Maritime Transport and named *Hong Qi 119*. She was renamed *Zhan Dou 51* in 1985.
  These two photographs must be products of my last visits to the Royal Docks in early 1970.

Glenorchy (ex-*Antenor*), built 1957, 7,974 tons. Glen. King George V Dock.
Built on the Tyne by Vickers Armstrong, she was transferred from Blue Funnel in 1970 and returned to them as the *Dymas* in 1972. This is another example of a ship being sold in 1973 to Macau/Somali interests but, in this case, she was sold on to Panamanian interests in 1976. She was broken up in China in 1983.

Breconshire, built 1942, 9,061 tons. Glen Line. Royal Albert.
Built by Robb Caledon, she had originally been ordered by Blue Funnel. Requisitioned on the stocks in 1941, she became the escort carrier HMS *Activity*, seeing service on Atlantic and Arctic convoys and from August 1944 in the Far East. She was sold to Glen Line in 1946 and scrapped in 1967.
   This photograph must have been taken in the last year, if not months, of her working life.

Glengarry (ex-*Empire Humber*), built 1940, 9,113 tons. Glen Line, King George V Dock.
As sister to the *Glenroy*, she was built by the Danish Burmeister & Wain and captured by the Germans in 1940 when Denmark was occupied. She was used initially as the U-boat depot ship *Meersburg* before being commissioned into the German navy as the commerce raider *Hansa*. She was recaptured at Kiel in 1945 and allocated the name *Empire Humber* by the Ministry of War Transport. She eventually became the *Glengarry* in 1946. Transferred to Blue Funnel as the *Dardanus* in 1970, she reverted to her original name prior to being scrapped in Japan in 1971.

Glengyle, built 1940, 9,095 tons. Glen Line, King George V.
Another sister to the *Glenroy* and also built by Caledon, she was requisitioned by the Admiralty after her launch and used initially as a fast supply ship. In 1940 she was converted to become an infantry landing ship, serving with distinction in numerous amphibious operations in the Mediterranean theatre. Her final war service was under the Australian Naval Board in the Far East. She was returned to Glen Line in 1946 and broken up in 1971.

Flintshire, built 1962, 11,926 tons. Glen Line. King George V.
The *Flintshire* was one of a batch of four sister ships delivered in 1962. Typical of the newer ships, she was some 40 feet longer than the other ships in the fleet and also faster, capable of 20 knots. At the same time, the traditional profile, particularly the tall, vertical funnel, was largely retained. She was also an example of another unfortunate rising trend in the early 1960s, wherein British shipping companies were buying ships or building ships abroad. While two of her sisters were built by Fairfields on the Clyde, the *Flintshire* was built in the Netherlands. She was sold in 1978 and scrapped in Taiwan in May 1979.

Above: *Surrey Trader*, built 1964, 14,064 tons. Trader Navigation. King George V.
By the standards of the time she was a rather large tramp steamer at double the normal gross
tonnage. Indeed, despite the cargo-handling gear, a ship-spotting website describes her as a bulker.
Built by Austin & Pickerskill, Sunderland, she was sold in 1970 and eventually scrapped in Xingang
in 1985.

Opposite above: *Glenlyon*, built 1962, 11,918 tons. Glen, Lyon. King George V Dock.
Sister to the *Flintshire*, she was also built in the Netherlands and sold to Singapore to become the
Emerald Express in 1978.

Opposite below: *Pembrokeshire*, built 1967, 13,300 tons. Glen Line. Royal Albert.
One of four ships, with two being built in Japan, for Glen Line. A further four were also built
for Blue Funnel. All four ships were fast (21 knots) and well equipped for handling conventional
cargoes. Transferred to Blue Funnel as the *Phrontis* in 1972, she was sold for further trading in
1982 to become the *Gulf Osprey* and then, a year later, the Iranian *Iran Ejtehad*. As the *Dophin VIII*
she was scrapped at Gadani Beach in 1995 after only eighteen years' service.
    It is a reflection on the rapidly changing times and serious lack of management foresight (Henri
Fayol's *prevoyance*) that both the Flintshire class and the Pembrokeshire classes had very short
lives. Both types were effectively out of date from the very beginning of their lives.

Markhor, built 1963, 6,867 tons. Brocklebank Line. Royal Albert.
Built by Alexander Stephen, she was transferred to Cunard-Brocklebank in 1968. Sold to Eggar
Forrester in 1976 after a period of lay-up in the River Fal, she was sold in 1981 to become the
Panamanian *Kara Unicorn* and broken up in Dalien in 1984.

Bulgaria (ex-*Empire Flamborough*), 1946, 4,191 tons. Bulgaria. Royal Albert.
One of the British-built war standards, built by Pickersgill in Sunderland in 1946. She became the
Bulgaria in 1948, remaining in service until 1976, when she was scrapped at Split in Croatia.

Federal/NZ/Avenue

Rakaia (ex-*Empire Abercorn*), built 1945, 8,563 tons. Federal/NZ Line. Royal Albert.
New Zealand Line had been founded by local farmers and traders in Christchurch (NZ) in 1873.
Historically, their ships could be identified by their pale buff funnels. In the 1960s this was replaced with the Federal red and black and house flag motif.

The *Rakaia* was built by Harland & Wolff in Belfast as one of nine upgraded standard tramp steamers, equipped with 420,000 cubic feet of refrigerated capacity. She became the *Rakaia* in 1946 and was scrapped in Hong Kong in 1971.

The NZ Line gave their ships Maori names. Rakaia is a township, river and gorge in New Zealand.

Antrim, built 1962, 6,461 tons. Avenue Shipping. Royal Albert.
Avenue Shipping was established in 1954 to operate the non-refrigerated ships of Federal/NZ Line.
The ships were named after Irish counties. It was a small but profitable part of the vast P&O empire, which disappeared into the P&O General Cargo division in the early 1970s. The *Antrim* was built on the Clyde and survived the P&O reorganisations until renamed *Strathinch* in 1975. She was sold in 1977 to Bangladeshi interests and then took on Hong Kong ownership. It was in this latter guise that she was wrecked on the west coast of South Korea in 1982 and broken up at Inchon.

Dorset, built 1949, 10,108 tons. Federal/NZ Line. Royal Albert.

Federal Line traced its origins back to 1895. From 1904 it operated a joint service with Houlder Bros to Australia and New Zealand. It was taken over by New Zealand Line in 1916 but continued to trade as a separate concern. The same year, NZ Line was taken over by P&O.

Federal Line ships were named for English counties. The *Dorset* was built by Alexander Stephen on the Clyde to replace an earlier *Dorset* lost during Second World War. She was transferred to P&O in the great reorganisation in 1971 and scrapped in 1972.

Somerset, built 1962, 7,602 tons. Federal/NZ Line. Royal Albert.

Built on the Clyde and transferred to P&O in 1973 as part of the great reorganisation. She was sold to Greece to become the *Aegean Sky* in 1980.

Paparoa, built 1944, 10,006 tons. Federal/NZ Line. Royal Albert.
She was built by Alexander Stephens at Linthouse on the Clyde but not as part of the 'Empire' programme. She was one of the five Papanui class sisters built to replace the heavy wartime losses. She was broken up in 1970.

Suffolk, built 1939, 11,145 tons. Federal/NZ Line. Royal Albert.
Built by John Brown on the Clyde, she was the third of three sister ships that were regarded as some of the finest long-distance cargo liners of the day. She was broken up at Kaohsiung in October 1968.
This is something of a classic view with three ships in line along the north quay of the Royal Albert Dock.

Taupo, built 1966, 10,983 tons. Federal/NZ Line. Royal Albert.
One of a class of four, three were given NZ Line Maori names and all were built by Bartrams of Sunderland. The fourth ship, built by Lithgows, took a Federal Line county name. She had a stylish new look; she was not particularly bigger, but she was faster at 20 knots. By this time, black hulls had been replaced by a rather attractive light green, while bipod masts and crane derricks had replaced traditional kingposts. She survived long enough into the grand P&O reorganisation to sport the new corporate colours of a light blue funnel with P&O inscribed on it, along with a buff hull and blue boot topping. She was sold in 1980 to become the *Mandama* and broken up at Kaohsuing in 1984.

Manapouri, built 1968, 12,691. Federal/NZ Line.
Built by Mitsui Zosen, she was obviously brand new and sporting the light green hull colour when photographed. She was named for a small town in the Fjordland area of south-west South Island. In 1977 she was sold to become the *Wild Martin*, then becoming the *Marathon Reefer* in 1982, the *Corfu Reefer* in 1987 and finally the *Limon Trader* in 1990. She was broken up at Alang in December 1999. Demolition did not actually start until the 25th, so it is likely that her broken hull survived into the year 2000.

Clan Line

The Clan Line was founded in Liverpool in 1877 by Charles Cayzer and operated a passenger service between the UK and India via the Suez Canal. The company became Cayzer, Irvine & Co. in 1879 and then Clan Line Association of Steamers in 1881, based in Glasgow, becoming the Clan Line of Steamers in 1890. In 1894 the company expanded into the Persian Gulf and North America, and began to carry cargo. The original Cayzer family retained overall control of the company. By the 1930s, the company had become the largest cargo-carrying concern in the world.

In 1956, Clan Line was merged with Union-Castle to form British & Commonwealth Shipping Ltd. In the 1970s, the group moved away from shipping into financial services. Clan Line effectively ceased to exist in 1981.

Clan Macdonald, built 1939, 8,141 tons. Clan Line. Royal Albert.
Built on the Clyde at Greenock in 1939, she was requisitioned as a landing ship by the Admiralty in 1940. Returned to Clan Line in 1948, she was broken up in Shanghai in 1970.

Clan Ramsay, built 1965, 10,542 tons. Clan Line. King George V.
Despite the problems in the UK shipbuilding industry at the time, she and her sisters were built at Greenock. She was actually owned by Union-Castle, effectively one of their 'R' class refrigerated ships. In 1977 she was renamed *Winchester Castle* and later *Winchester Universal*, before being sold to Greece in 1980.

Clan Macnab, built 1961, 9,428 tons. Clan Line. Royal Albert.
Also built at Greenock, she was sold in 1980 to Panama to become the *New Eagle*.
  I always had a soft spot for the *Clan Macnab*. I was privileged to visit her when she was loading for her maiden voyage and later wrote about my adventure in the school magazine.

Moldanger, built 1950, 8,055 tons. Westfal-Larsen, Norway. King George V Dock.
December 1968, and a somewhat gloomy winter scene in the King George V Dock.

Ellerman

The Ellerman Line was founded during the nineteenth century and expanded largely by acquisition to become one of the largest shipping companies in the world, trading globally. My 1967 edition of *Ocean Ships* describes the routes as too numerous to give in detail. Despite the ravages of war, in the mid-1950s the fleet consisted of ninety-four ships; there were still fifty-nine in the early 1960s. All these ships had been built post-war.

In the 1960s Ellerman joined the Associated Container Transport Group and started the successful containerisation of the Mediterranean services. There was also close working with the Scottish Ben Line, with a number of ships transferred between the two fleets. During the 1970s the company diversified its activities. The business was sold in 1983 and the shipping activities eventually became part of Trafalgar House in the form of Cunard-Ellerman. This was sold to the Andrew Weir Group and then on to the German Hamburg-Sud in 2003. By 2004 Ellerman ceased to exist.

City of Winchester, built 1952, 10,594 tons. Ellerman Lines.
Another action shot – entering the Royal Docks from the river. She was built by Denny of Dumbarton, before becoming the Ben Lines *Benvannoch* in 1970 and being broken up in Kaohsiung in 1975.

Close examination of the bow will reveal that the figurehead was frequently the coat of arms of the city or town for which the ship was named.

City of Birmingham, built 1949, 7,599 tons. Ellerman Lines. Royal Albert.
One of the ten-ship City of Oxford class of cargo liner ordered from six different UK yards. Built by John Brown, Clydebank, she remained with Ellerman all her working life until scrapped in October 1971. She was the only one of the class not sold for further trading.

City of Canberra, built 1961, 10,543 tons. Ellerman Line. Royal Albert.
One of five ships, she was built by Barclay Curle for the Australian service. She was sold in 1977 to become the Singaporean *Tasgold* and broken up in Kaohsiung in November 1979.
   This view demonstrates well the trend towards moving the superstructure further aft. This class was the first ships designed three quarters aft to be built for Ellerman Lines.

City of Chester, built 1944, 8,380 tons. Ellerman Line. Royal Albert.
Built by Barclay Curle in Glasgow. Despite the date, she was not part of the wartime Empire programme. She was scrapped in Hong Kong in 1971. At the time this photograph was taken, she had become the oldest ship in the Ellerman Line fleet and actually outlived some of the newer ships.

City of Eastbourne, built 1962, 10,006 tons. Ellerman Line. Royal Albert.
The 'city' honoured in the ship's name did not have to be a city! Eastbourne was honoured because of the Ellerman long-term family connections. A previous *City of Eastbourne* had been built in 1923 and was sold during the 1950s. A sister to the *City of Canberra*, this one was built by Vickers Armstrong on the Tyne. She was switched to the Canadian service and renamed *City of Toronto* in 1971, before being sold to Singapore in 1978 where she became the *Kota Cantik*. She was eventually broken up in Kaohsiung in 1984.

City of Lancaster, built 1958, 4,949 tons. Ellerman.
Built by Swan Hunter at Wallsend, she was involved in a collision with the *Thistle Venture* in September 1979 and was broken up at San Esteban de Pravia in January 1982.

City of Poona, built 1946, 9,962 tons. Ellerman. King George V Dock.
Built by Swan Hunter, she was transferred to the Ben Line in 1968 as the *Benarkle* and broken up in Kaohsiung in 1974.

City of Exeter, built 1953, 13,345 tons. Ellerman. Royal Albert.
Built by Vickers Armstrong at the High Walker Naval Yard on Tyneside, she was one of a quartet of all first-class passenger cargo liners introduced on the East Africa run. As such, she was in competition with British India's slightly larger but slower *Kenya* and *Uganda*, Union-Castle's one-class round-Africa service and the Italian Lloyd Triestino. The latter's ships were much faster but smaller. Of the English ships in the trade, the Ellerman liners were regarded as the best and as first choice by many prospective travellers.

Sold to Greece in 1971, she was converted to become a ro-ro ferry on the Patras–Brindisi–Ancona service and was eventually scrapped at Aliaga in 1998.

City of Glasgow, built 1963, 10,017 tons. Ellerman. Royal Albert.
A sister ship to the *City of Eastbourne*, she was also by Vickers Armstrong in Newcastle. In 1971 she was transferred to the Canadian service and appropriately renamed *City of Ottawa*. With her sister she was sold to Pacific International Lines of Singapore to become the *Kota Cahaya* in 1978 and broken up in Nantong 1985.

City of Gloucester, built 1963, 4,961 tons. Ellerman. Royal Albert.
Built by Denny's in Dumbarton, she was sold in 1979 and renamed *Suete*, before being scrapped in 1985. In those days we were still exporting railway rolling stock, as illustrated by the deck cargo.

City of Johannesburg, built 1947, 8,207 tons. Ellerman. King George V Dock.
When a ship was berthed at the extreme eastern end of the King George V Dock, a full side-on view was possible from the Royal Albert. The ship was built by Barclay Curle and differed from her sisters by being diesel driven rather than powered by steam turbines. This was done for comparison purposes. She was sold to Greece in 1970 and broken up in 1973.

City of Port Elizabeth, built 1952, 13,363 tons. Ellerman.
Another of the famous quartet of East Africa – all first-class liners built by Vickers Armstrong on the Tyne. She too was sold to Greece in 1971, with the view to being converted into a ro-ro or a cruise liner. Sadly neither project was progressed and she remained laid up until she was scrapped in 1980.

City of York, built 1953, 13,345 tons. Ellerman Lines. Royal Albert.
Evening shadows are lengthening at the end of a cold but bright day in February 1970. This picture shows well the fine lines of these four sister ships. Like her sisters, she was built by Vickers Armstrong. She was sold in 1971 to Karageorgis of Greece to become the *Mediterranean Sky*, operating on the ferry service across the Adriatic from Brindisi to Patras.

Due to the poor financial health of her owners, she was arrested in Patras in August 1996 at the end of a voyage from Brindisi. She was laid up at Patras until 1999, when she was towed to Eleusis. Laid up again, she began to take on water in late 2002 and she was beached and abandoned. She eventually capsized in shallow water in January 2003; the wreck is still partially visible. A sad end to a very fine ship.

Niceto de Larrinaga, built 1959, 7,292 tons. Larrinaga. Royal Albert.
Typical tramp steamer built by Shorts in Sunderland, caught on a somewhat miserable day. She was sold to Greece in 1972 and then to Far Eastern buyers in 1978, before being broken up in Kaohsiung in 1981.

Pretoria, built 1952, 8,621 tons. East Asiatic, Denmark. Royal Albert.
Despite wartime conditions, the East Asiatic Co. embarked on a new building programme, which eventually materialised as a group of seventeen ships divided into three distinct classes. Five formed the 'P' class. Built in Denmark, she was sold and renamed *Bering Sea* in 1972 and acquired Somali registry. She was sold again in 1974 to China, probably for scrapping. The four surviving 'P' class ships had all been scrapped by 1983.

Slesvig, built 1959, 13,393 tons. Dansk-Fransk, Denmark. King George V Dock.
Built in Lubeck and described on the web as a 'bulker', she is clearly discharging some kind of bulk cargo. She was sold in 1974 to become the *Arkadia* and again in 1982 to become the *Diogenes*. She was eventually broken up in Fuzhou in July 1986.

P&O/British India

P&O owes its origins to the establishment in 1835 of a regular steamer service from London to Spain and Portugal. As such, it was probably the first true steamship-operated liner service, antedating Samuel Cunard by five years. The famous house flag owes its origin to the blue-and-white flag of the Portuguese kingdom and the red-and-yellow of Spain. A mail contract serving Iberia was awarded in 1837 and a further mail contract was awarded in 1840 to deliver mail to Alexandria in Egypt. The company, Peninsular & Oriental Steam Navigation, was incorporated by Royal Charter in 1840.

The company grew to be a major shipping line and passenger liner operator. British India Line (formed originally in 1856 as the Calcutta & Burmah Steam Navigation Company and, becoming British India SN 1862), was taken over in 1914; a controlling interest was acquired in the Orient Line in 1918. Both companies continued to operate as separate entities until the 1960s. Orient Line was merged into P&O in 1960 and subsequent refits saw the disappearance of the attractive corn-coloured hulls.

Ballarat, built 1954, 8,792 tons. P&O. King George V Dock.
A fast (18 knots) freighter built by Alexander Stephen for the Australian wool trade. She had a bale capacity of 683,500 cubic feet. She was also equipped for heavy cargo handling, with one 80-ton and two 15-ton booms. Renamed *Pando Cape* as part of P&O's corporate image exercise, she was then sold to Ben Line to become the *Benledi* and was broken up at Inchon in 1978.

Even in the mid-1960s, when change and competition were beginning to make serious inroads, P&O and British India owned around sixty-five ships between them, making them one of the largest fleets to use the Royal and Tilbury docks regularly.

In 1969 P&O became part of Oversea Containers Limited, eventually buying out all its partners by 1986. By this time all its cargo operations had been converted to containerisation. In 1972 the companies such as Avenue, Stick Line, Federal/NZ and Hain-Norse, which had operated as separate entities, were all absorbed into the P&O Group and corporate identity.

The shipping activities were eventually merged with Nedlloyd and later acquired by the Maersk Group.

Some remnants of the P&O Group can still be seen along the River Thames. A vehicle carrying ferry service from Antwerp still operates, and the ships sport a dark-blue funnel with the famous house flag displayed on it.

Baradine (ex-*Nardana*), built 1956, 8,511 tons. P&O. King George V Dock.
Originally one of four 'N' class ships built for the British India Line's East Africa and Australian routes. She was transferred to P&O in 1963. She reverted to her old name when she returned to British India and survived to become briefly part of P&O's General Cargo Division. She was sold to Iran in 1973 and broken up at Gadani Beach in 1976.

Chakla (ex-*Swiftpool*), built 1954, 6,565 tons. British India. Royal Albert.
Built by Robb Caledon, Dundee, she was acquired from Pool Shipping in 1964 and survived to become part of the P&O General Cargo Division in 1971. She was sold to Singapore to become the *Golden Bear* in 1972 and was broken up in Kaohsuing in 1975.

Chantala, built 1950, 7,556 tons. British India. Royal Albert.
Built by Barclay Curle, she was a cadet training ship in the BI fleet. A total of 769 cadets received their training on her. Badly damaged in a collision on the Thames in 1969, she was sold in 1971 to Singapore and broken up in China three years later.

Chilka, built 1950, 7,087 tons. British India. Royal Albert.
Built by Swan Hunter at the Neptune Yard, Low Walker. After an uneventful life, she was broken up in Kaohsiung in 1972.

Chinkoa, built 1952, 7,102 tons. British India. King George V Dock.
Built by Barclay Curle. Badly damaged in bad weather at Antwerp in the spring of 1972, she was scrapped at Bilbao in Spain later that year.

Chitral (ex-*Jadotville*), built 1956, 13,809 tons. P&O. King George V Dock.
One of the last passenger ships built for Cie Maritime Belge, she and her sister were sold for a knock-down bargain price of £3 million to P&O following Congolese independence in 1960. She operated from London to the Far East, before transferring to service from Australia to the Far East and Japan in 1970. She was scrapped in 1975.

Coromandel, built 1949, 7,065 tons. P&O. Royal Albert.
Built by Barclay Curle, she was sold in 1969 to Hong Kong and later re-registered in Singapore. Following a lay-up period in Manila and being driven ashore in June 1972 by typhoon Konsing, she was sold to Somalia in 1973 but then scrapped in Taiwan later the same year.

Kenya, built 1951, 14,464 tons. British India. Royal Albert.

Apart from the troopship *Nevasa*, the *Kenya* and her famous sister the *Uganda* were the largest ships operated by British India before they moved into large tankers. Photographed in dry dock adjacent to the Royal Albert in 1966, she was a reminder that, despite increased competition from air travel, it was still possible to travel by sea from London to East Africa in style and comfort in the mid-1960s. However, rapid political and economic changes soon brought an end to this service. This elegant and popular ship was sold for scrapping at La Spezia in 1969.

Nowshera, built 1955, 8,516 tons. British India. Royal Albert.

A typical 1960s scene, with lines of ships along the north quay of the Royal Albert. Another of the 'N' class, the *Nowshera* was built by Scotts of Greenock and survived long enough to become briefly part of the P&O General Cargo Division, before being sold to Iran to become the *Ayra Chehr* in 1973. She was broken up in Shanghai in 1976.

Purnea, built 1947, 5,340 tons. British India. Royal Albert.
Another typical 1960s scene in the Royal Albert, with some of the numerous barges that were used to transfer cargoes to and from the ocean-going ships. The *Purnea* was broken up in Spain in 1971.

Salmara, built 1956, 8,199 tons. P&O. King George V Dock.
A reefer ship built by John Brown. I must have caught this one before the first of her many changes of name! After becoming the *Arakawa* in 1966, the *Teesta* in 1970 and the *Strathloyal*, complete with new corporate P&O light-blue hull and funnel colours in 1975. She was eventually broken up at Gadani Beach in 1978.

Apparently, from quite early on in her life she had a bad reputation for engine breakdowns.

Above and below: *Salsette*, built 1956, 8,199 tons. P&O.
A refrigerated ship built by John Brown at Clydebank, she served both P&O and British India until she was sold in 1967. Like her sister the *Salmara*, she also had a bad reputation for engine breakdowns. She is shown in the King George V Dock sporting P&O (black funnel) colours and in the Royal Albert sporting British India (black with two white bands close together) colours.

Soudan, built 1948, 9,080 tons. P&O. King George V Dock.
Another typical 1960s scene, this time on the north side of the King George V dock. The *Soudan* was built by Barclay Curle as a fast (18 knots) cargo liner for the Far East service. She was broken up in Taiwan in 1970.

Uganda, built 1952, 14,430 tons. British India. Royal Albert.
Probably the most famous ship in this whole gallery! Built by Barclay Curle, she was the 450th ship to join the British India fleet. In 1966 it was still just possible to make the seventeen-night voyage from London to Mombasa. However in January 1967 she was withdrawn from the East Africa run and converted in Germany to become a school ship providing educational cruises. It was in this role in Alexandria on 10 April 1982 that she was requisitioned for hospital duties in the Falklands War. Ordered to Naples to offload the school children, she was sent to Gibraltar for conversion and then off to the Falklands, where she gave heroic service. She returned to Southampton in August 1982 to a rousing welcome. She was retained on charter to the British government for a further two years before being laid up at Falmouth. The school cruise market was in terminal decline so, despite preservation efforts, she was sold for scrapping in Taiwan in 1986.

She may well have just completed her last voyage as a conventional passenger liner when this picture was taken.

Above and below: *Sunda/Pando Strait*, built 1952, 9,235 tons. P&O. King George V Dock.
Amid the organisational changes taking place during the late 1960s, it became inevitable that a ship would appear twice, albeit under a different name.

Originally built by John Brown, Clydebank, in 1953 she rescued the British India *Chinkoa* at Gibralter and towed her back to Falmouth for repairs. In April 1961 she was involved in two collisions in the English Channel. On dry docking at Southampton she then hit the dockyard gates!

Under the new corporate restyling for P&O Lines, she became the *Pando Strait*. As part of the General Cargo Division, she was sold for scrapping at Inverkeithing in 1972.

She appears in both guises, the latter while dry docked at the western end of the Royal Albert.

Strathardle, built 1967, 13,057 tons. P&O. King George V Dock.
She was built by Mitsui Zosan in Japan for the UK–Far Eastern service. She and her sisters were marketed as the 'Super Straths'. They were fast (21 knots) and stylish. Later she was transferred to the Persian Gulf–Japan service, replacing withdrawn British India 'N' class ships. She and her sisters survived in the P&O General Cargo Division long enough to receive the new blue corporate colours. She was sold to become the Thai-owned *Anchan* in 1979 and eventually scrapped in Huangpo in 1986.

Strathbora, built 1967, 12, 539 tons. P&O. Royal Albert.
Built in Japan, she was sold in 1979 to Thailand for further trading as the *Benjamas* before being scrapped at Kaohsiung in 1986.

Strathconon, built 1967, 12,800 tons. P&O. Royal Albert.
She was sold in 1979 to Thailand as the *Chuangchou* but became stranded in the Red Sea in May 1980. Salvaged and repaired by new Greek owners, she operated as the *Tzelepi* before being broken up in Shanghai in 1984.

Hoegh Augvlad, built 1958, 8,292 tons. Hoegh, Norway. Royal.
Built at Uddevalla in Sweden, this Norwegian-owned tramp steamer was scrapped in 1981.

Bennevis (ex-*Bardic*, 1959, ex-*Muncaster Castle*, 1954, ex-HMS *Puncher*), built 1944, 7,994 tons. Ben Line. Royal Albert.

It was unusual to see Ben Line steamers in the Royal Docks. This image, taken in the spring of 1966, presents a very active picture of the Royal Docks, with a tug moving, barges around the ships and Union-Castle and Brocklebank Line ships berthed at adjacent quays.

Ordered as a C3 class freighter with the Seattle-Tacoma Shipbuilding Corporation in Tacoma (Wash), she was completed as an escort aircraft carrier and delivered after modification to the Royal Navy under the Lend-Lease agreement. She was crewed by Canadians and served with distinction on the Russian convoys. Returned to the US at the end of the war, she was paid off and sold to UK owners. She was eventually scrapped in Taiwan in 1973.

Union-Castle

Union-Castle Line owed its origins to a merger in December 1899 between the Union Line, formed in 1853, and the Castle Packets Co., dating from 1876.

Above and below: *Braemar Castle*, built 1952, 17,029 tons. Union-Castle. King George V Dock.
Rhodesia Castle, built 1951, 17,051 tons. Union-Castle. King George V.
The *Braemar Castle* was one of my first London photographs in October 1965. She was the third of three sisters built by Harland & Woolf for the Union-Castle one-class round-Africa service, which was regarded as somewhat inferior to that offered by Ellerman, British India and particularly Lloyd Triestino. The decline and eventual demise of this service due to competition from air travel, political and economic changes led to both ships being scrapped in 1968 after very short working lives.

Kenya Castle, built 1952, 17,041 tons. Union-Castle. King George V.
The second of the round-Africa trio built by Harland & Wolff, she was withdrawn from the East
Africa service in 1966 and, unlike her sisters, was laid up. She was sold in 1967 to the Greek
Chandris Line to become the *Amerikanis* and was converted to a cruising liner. Apart from a
two-year charter with the Italian Costa Line, she served with Chandris until 1996. Eventually,
she was scrapped at Alangi in India in 2001 after a working life three times that of her two sisters.

At forty-nine years, this must make her one of the longest serving ships in this collection.

Tantallon Castle, built 1954, 7,432 tons. Union-Castle. King George V Dock.
Built by Harland & Wolff. The post-war Union-Castle freighters did not have the lavender-grey hull colour. She was sold to Cyprus to become the *Aris II* in 1971 and was broken up in Japan in 1978.

El Gezira, built 1964, 3,212 tons. Sudan Line, Sudan. Royal Albert.
Another example of the effects of the wind of change. African countries were acquiring their own fleets. The *El Gezira* remained with Sudan Line until 1980.

Port Line

In 1914 the Commonwealth & Dominion Line was formed from four smaller companies operating twenty-three ships on the Australia and New Zealand run. It was taken over by Cunard in 1916 and took the distinctive Cunard funnel colours after the First World War. The 'Port' prefix began to appear with new ships after the First World War and the company, always known as the 'Port Line', was officially branded as Port Line Limited in November 1937.

A founder member of Associated Container transport in January 1966, the last conventional Port Line ships were transferred to Brocklebank Line in 1982.

Port Launceston, built 1957, 8,957 tons. Port Line. King George V Dock.
Built by Harland & Wolff in Belfast, she was sold in 1977 to Woburn Shipping of Singapore, becoming the *United Vantage*. She was broken up in Kaohsiung in 1980.

Port Auckland, built 1949, 11,845 tons. Port Line. King George V.
Built by Hawthorn Leslie on the Tyne, the *Port Auckland* was a very stylish, modern-looking ship, way ahead of her time in many ways. She was sold to become a sheep carrier on the Australia–Arabian Gulf service in 1976 and broken up in Kaohsuing in 1979.

Port Hobart (ex-*Empire Wessex*), built 1946, 11,149 tons. Port Line. Royal Albert.
It is always a refreshing change to photograph a ship on the move, even if it is from the stern. Built by Harland & Wolff as a tramp and upgraded to a fast refrigerated ship, she had 490,000 cubic feet of refrigerated space. She was broken up in Shanghai in August 1970.

Port Littleton, built 1947, 7,413 tons. Port Line. Royal Albert.
Another action shot, probably taken lying down to avoid the mooring ropes! Built by Hawthorn
Leslie at Hebburn, she was broken up at Faslane in 1972 after an uneventful life.

Port New Plymouth, built 1960, 13,085 tons. Port Line. Royal Albert.
Another extremely stylist addition to the Port Line fleet, again way ahead of her contemporaries in
looks and elegance. Built by Swan Hunter, she was at the time the largest and possibly the fastest
(18 knots) of the Port Line refrigerated ships. Still in her prime at the end of the 1960s, she held out
against the container revolution until she was broken up in Kaohsiung in 1979.

Port Pirie, built 1947, 10,535 tons. Port Line. King George V.
Built by Swan Hunter at Wallsend, she was reputed to be haunted and she had particularly unreliable engines. After an unglamorous life, she was broken up at Castellon in Spain in 1972.

Port Chalmers, built 1968, 16,283 tons. Port Line. King George V.
Built on the Clyde, it was amazing that, even as late as 1968, traditional refrigerated cargo ships were still being built. She epitomised the bigger and faster (over 21 knots) traditional philosophy. She became the Brocklebank liner *Manaar* in 1981 and the *Golden Glory* in 1983, before being scrapped in 1985 after a relatively short life of only seventeen years.

Designed to accommodate palletised cargo, she was devoid of sheer and, comparing her with some of her sisters of earlier years, she seemed to represent a retrograde step in both style and looks. Despite being already half way to being a container ship, she was not considered worth converting.

Japanese Miscellany

Momijisan Maru, built 1959, 9,548 tons. Mitsui/OSK, Japan. Royal Albert.
Built by Mitsui, she was one of the last pair of an eighteen-ship post-war reconstruction programme. The eight 'M' class ships were built between 1956 and 1959. Sold in 1973 and again in 1978, she was finally scrapped as the *Han Garan* at Pusan in 1984.

Barcelona Maru, built 1967, 10,463 tons. Mitsui/OSK, Japan. Royal Albert.
One of a class of four fast freighters, capable of over 20 knots, built by Mitsui in Kobe. Not converted to a container ship, she was sold to Iran in 1983 and eventually scrapped at Alang in 1998, having outlived all her sisters by fifteen years.

When Mitsui and OSK merged, they took on a neutral corporate colour scheme. The orange funnel and blue hull with green boot topping is the dubious result.

Royal Miscellany I

Vishva Prabha, built 1959, 9,460 tons. SCI, India. King George V.
Built at Pula in Yugoslavia, she traded between India and Western Europe. In January 1981 she ran aground near Tripoli. Refloated, she was considered not worth repairing so she was sold for breaking up in Spilt, not far from her birthplace.

This illustrates another aspect of the wind of change blowing through the British shipping industry. Independent countries were establishing their own fleets to compete with those of the colonial powers. The Shipping Corporation of India is a government of Indian enterprise. Established in 1961 by amalgamating two small companies, it has grown into a major corporation with a $580-million turnover and a fleet tonnage of 5.9 million tons deadweight.

State of Kerala, built 1957, 9,004 tons. India. Royal Albert.
Built in Sweden by Kockums of Malmo as the Norwegian-flagged *Bernhard*, she was sold to India in 1962. After an uneventful career, she was scrapped at Bombay (Mumbai) in 1982.

Indian Strength, built 1958, 7,185 tons. Indian Steamship, India. Royal Albert.
Built in Germany, she was sold in 1979 to another Indian operator before being sold again in 1981 to become the *Success* under the Panamanian flag. Caught up in the Gulf conflicts she was sunk as the result of a missile attack in the Persian Gulf in 1981.

Oakbank, built 1963, 6,308 tons. Bank Line. Royal Victoria.
Bank Line had a post-war strategy of maintaining a fleet of around fifty tween deck general-cargo freighters. A large order for thirty-eight such ships was shared between Harland & Wolff and William Doxford of Sunderland. The Oakbank was one of the Sunderland ships. She was sold in 1978 to become the *Good Spirit* and again in 1984 to become the *Discovery,* before being broken up at Alang in India in 1985.

Castagnola, built 1961, 8,673 tons. Switzerland, King George V Dock.
The only claim to fame or comment this ship has was that she was Swiss! At the time, there were about thirty ships plying the oceans that flew the Swiss flag and were usually registered in Basle. It would appear that at the time she was under charter to Burma Five Star Line.

Cotopaxi, built 1954, 8,559 tons. Pacific SN. Royal Albert.
Built at Denny's in Dumbarton on the Clyde, she was one of a batch of six ships built for both Clan Line and Pacific Steam Navigation. She was sold to Greece in 1973 and scrapped in China in 1975.

Fineo, built 1951, 6,702 tons. Ligure di Armamento Genova, Italy. King George V Dock.
Stylish-looking Italian tramp steamer, eventually sold in 1969.

Egoro, Norway.
A Norwegian tramp steamer observed heading up the Thames, towards either the West India or
Surrey Commercial docks. This is a real action photograph taken from the Woolwich Ferry in the
autumn of 1969.

Shaw Savill

The Shaw Savill Line dated originally from 1858, trading to Australia and New Zealand. In 1928 it was bought out by the White Star Line. Following the merger with Cunard, White Star gave up the Australia and New Zealand services. Despite being under the control of Furness Withy, Shaw Savill retained its separate identity and also two classic White Star features: the buff funnel with the black top and names ending in '-ic'. It will be evident that many classic and famous White Star names reappeared under the Shaw Savill banner.

Above: *Alaric*, built 1958, 6,692 tons. Shaw Savill. King George V Dock.
Built by Harland & Wolff in Glasgow, she differed from her three German-built sisters in having refrigerated cargo space. She was sold to Iran in 1972 and eventually broken up in Bombay in 1979.

Opposite above: *Argentina* (ex-*President Peron*), built 1950, 12,627 tons. ELMA, Argentina. Royal Albert.
Built to inaugurate a Buenos Aires–London service, she was converted to a cargo ship in 1967. In 1969 she was laid up at Rosario before being scrapped at Campana in 1973. Photographed in February 1966, she was in her last year as a traditional passenger liner.

Opposite below: *Libertad* (ex-*17 de Octubre*), built 1950, 12,653 tons. ELMA, Argentina. Royal Albert.
She was laid up in 1974 at Villa Constitución and scrapped at Campana in 1975. These two ships, along with a third – the *Uruguay* (ex-*Eva Peron*) – operated the passenger service from London and other European ports to South America until the mid-1960s. It is not just sales, transfer or reorganisations that give rise to name changes; political changes motivated these cases.

Arabic, built 1956, 6,553 tons. Shaw Savill. Royal Albert.
The fourth ship to carry this name. The first had been operated by White Star from 1881 to 1901. The second was acquired in 1902 and sank in 1915, while the third came as reparations, having been the NDL *Berlin*. This latter ship was eventually broken up in Genoa in 1931.

This ship was one of three sisters built by Bremer Vulkan and, being non-refrigerated, was used primarily in the wool trade. She was transferred in 1968 within the Furness Withy Group to become the Pacific SN *Oroya* and later the *Pacific Ranger*. She was sold in 1972 to Hong King Islands Shipping and was eventually scrapped at Inchon in 1983.

Aramaic, built 1957, 6,553 tons. Shaw Savill. King George V Dock.
A long view of the King George V dock, with Port, Ellerman and Glen liners further down the quay, taken from just inside the dock gates. German-built like her sister the *Arabic*, she was transferred to Pacific SN to become the *Oropesa*. She too was sold in 1972 to Hong Kong and scrapped in 1983.

Canopic, built 1954, 11,166 tons. Shaw Savill. King George V Dock.
Built by Vickers Armstrong, she was one of five 'C' class refrigerator ships. The onset of the containerisation of traffic saw her transferred to the Cairn Line in 1973 before being sold to Cypriot interests in 1975. She was eventually broken up Aliaga in 1986, the last of the five sisters to be scrapped.
   White Star also operated a *Canopic* from 1903 to 1925.

Carnatic, built 1956, 11,144 tons. Shaw Savill. Royal Albert.
Built by Cammell Laird at Birkenhead, she was the last of the five 'C' sisters and. like the *Canopic*, had more insulated refrigerated capacity than the earlier sisters. She became the *Darro* (Royal Mail Lines) in 1973 before being sold in 1977 and eventually broken up at Kaohsiung in 1979.
   Film buffs will recognise the name from the film *Around the World in Eighty Days*.

Delphic, built 1949, 10,691 tons. Shaw Savill. Royal Albert.
One of the first of the post-war reconstruction programme, she was built by Hawthorn Leslie. She was broken up in Kaohsiung in 1971. To add insult to injury, she had already been registered as owned by Overseas Container Lines.

There was a White Star *Delphic* in 1897 and a second one in 1925.

Doric, built 1949, 10,675 tons. Shaw Savill, King George V.
Sister to the *Delphic*, she was built by Fairfields of Govan. Not much more is known except that she was scrapped in 1969.

There was a White Star *Doric* from 1893 to 1911, and a later ship built in 1923 and scrapped at Newport, South Wales, in 1935.

Iberic, built 1961, 11,248 tons. Shaw Savill. Royal Albert.
Built by Alexander Stevens of Glasgow, she became the Royal Mail *Deseado* before being sold to become the *San George* (Greek flag) and scrapped at Chittagong in 1983.

Icenic, built 1960, 11,239 tons. Shaw Savill. Royal Albert.
Built by Harland & Woolf, she was sold to become the *Agean Unity* and subsequently was broken up in Kaohsiung in 1979.

Ionic, built 1959, 11,219 tons. Shaw Savill. Royal Albert.
Built by Cammell Laird at Birkenhead, she was sold and renamed *Glenparva*, flying the Cypriot flag, in 1978 and scrapped in 1979.

　　There was an *Ionic* from 1883, which was sold in 1900. A second *Ionic* was delivered in 1902 and served until 1936.

Illyric, built 1960, 11,256 tons. Shaw Savill. Royal Albert.
Built by Vickers Armstrong at High Walker, she was sold in 1977 to Ardgowan Shipping of Southampton and then on to Cypriot buyers in 1978, becoming the *Carmelia*. She was scrapped at Kaohsiung in March 1979.

Laurentic, built 1965, 7,964 tons. Shaw Savill, Royal Albert.
A refrigerated ship built by Vickers Armstrong at High Walker, she was sold to Greece in 1980 to become the *Spartan Reefer*. She was broken up at Gadani Beach in 1984.

A previous *Laurentic* was built by Harland & Wolff in 1909 and sunk by mine with heavy loss of life off the Irish coast in January 1917. She was carrying a substantial amount of gold and it is rumoured that not all of this has been recovered. A later ship built in 1927 was torpedoed in November 1940.

One change from the White Star tradition is evident. The black hull with the white line has been replaced by a light grey, although the white line is retained.

Megantic, built 1962, 12,226 tons. Shaw Savill. Royal Albert.
A refrigerated ship built by Swan Hunter at the Neptune Yard, Low Walker, she was the first Shaw Savill freighter to depart from the traditional White Star black hull. She was capable of 18 knots. She was sold to Greece in 1979 and scrapped at Kaohsiung in April 1980.

A previous White Star *Megantic* had been launched in 1908 and scrapped in Japan in 1933.

Persic, built 1949, 13,593 tons. Shaw Savill. Royal Albert.
When built by Cammel Laird, she was one of the largest refrigerated ships on the Australasian trade.
She was transferred to the Royal Mail Line in 1970 as the *Derwent* and scrapped in Bilbao in 1971.

An earlier *Persic* had been built in 1899 and, after serving with distinction in the First World War, was scrapped in 1927.

Suevic, built 1950, 13,587 tons. Shaw Savill. Royal Albert.
A sister to the *Persic*, she was built by Harland & Wolff and scrapped in 1974 after an engine failure.

An earlier *Suevic* was delivered in 1900. She was involved in a spectacular grounding on the Lizard in 1907. Salvaged, she was returned to service with White Star until she was sold in 1928 to Norway to become a whale factory ship. She was scuttled to avoid capture in 1942.

Waiwera, built 1944, 11,138 tons. Shaw Savill. Royal Albert.
Not all the Shaw Savill ships had traditional White Star '-ic' type names. Built by Harland & Wolff as one of the permitted civilian orders to replace an earlier war loss, she proved to be one of the prototypes of the standard fast Empire-type cargo boats built towards the end of the war. She was sold to Greece to become the *Julia* in 1967.

Zealandic, built 1965, 7,946 tons. Shaw Savill. Royal Albert.
A refrigerated ship built by Alexander Stephens, she spent some years under charter before being sold to Greek interests in 1980. She was later sold on to Liberian interests, becoming the *Khalij Crystal*, and eventually broken up at Gadani Beach in 1984.
  A White Star *Zealandic* was built in 1911, serving with distinction during the First World War. Sold in 1926, she was requisitioned as a decoy ship in 1939, and attacked and sunk off Cromer in 1941. A second *Zealandic* was sunk in 1941.

Royal Miscellany II

Havmoy, built 1953, 4,977 tons. Norway. Royal Albert.
Built in Gothenburg, Sweden, she was sold in 1967 to become the *Aud Presthus* and again in 1973 to become the *Hoe Seng*. After four further changes of name, she was eventually broken up in Bombay in 1982.

Lord Viking, built 1960, 4,641 tons. Norway. Royal Victoria.
Built at Drammen in Norway, she spent a substantial part of her life on charter to Canadian Pacific, even taking the funnel colours. She was sold to become the *Horizon* until 1980, when she became the *Cargo King*, still flying the Norwegian flag.

Medicine Hat. Norway Royal Albert.
Another typical example of a tramp steamer on a long-term liner charter again to Canadian Pacific.

Vibran Njord. Norway. Royal Albert.
Built at Gothenburg in Sweden, she started life as the *Langfonn*, becoming the *Vibran Njord* in 1964. In 1966 she briefly and temporarily became the *Concordia Vibran* (Haaland Line) before reverting to the name *Vibran Njord*. She eventually became the Cypriot *Houda Star*.

Loradore, built 1958, 8,077 tons. Michalinos. Royal Albert.
Built by William Gray, Hartlepool, she was sold in 1966 to become the *Aliartos* under the Panamanian flag. In 1970 she became the *Thomas A*, flying the Greek flag and was sold again in 1975 to become the *Irenes Banner*, still under the Greek flag. In 1978 she caught fire at Dawes Island near Port Harcourt; she was beached and declared a constructive total loss.

Aubade, built 1961, 14,861 tons. Panama. Royal Victoria.
Flags of convenience were not rare in the 1960s, but they were certainly in a minority.
   Described as a 1960s-built 'bulker', she is seen discharging grain into the massive elevators that dominated the south side of the Royal Victoria dock. She remained with the same owner and under the same flag for her entire working life.

Rosewood, built 1963, 10,694 tons. J. I. Jacobs. King George V Dock.
A rare action shot. As I was walking back to the dock gates, the bridge at the end of the King George V Dock opened and the *Rosewood* came through. It appears she was sold soon afterwards.

Andania, built 1960, 7,004 tons. Cunard. Royal Albert.
Like White Star, Cunard also perpetrated names, although many glamorous liner names eventually finished up on freighters. The previous *Andania* had been a passenger liner built in 1922 for the Canadian service, and was sunk in 1940. This ship was built by William Hamilton at Port Glasgow, also for the Canadian service, and was transferred to Brocklebank Line in 1970. She was sold to Chinese/Panama interests in 1971 and scrapped in 1986.

Saxonia, built 1964, 5,586 tons. Cunard. Royal Albert.
The previous *Saxonia* was built in 1954 for the Canadian service, before becoming a cruising liner. This ship was transferred to Brocklebank Line without an apparent change of name in 1970 and sold to Singapore in 1978.

Ibaraki Maru, built 1965, 9,923 tons. NYK, Japan. Royal Albert.
This was Japan's response to the fast freighter competition. One of two batches of four fast freighters, she was capable of 18 ¾ knots. The second batch were slightly longer and larger, and capable of 20 knots. Later Japanese freighters were capable of over 20. She was sold in 1978 to become the *Chan Ho*, becoming the *Selma* in 1983. It appears she was scrapped soon after.

Blue Funnel Line

Alfred Holt's Liverpool-based Blue Funnel Line was founded in 1865. They acquired the Glen Line in 1935, and the normal pattern was that Glen Line ships sailed from London, while Blue Funnel ships usually sailed from Glasgow, Liverpool and Swansea. To see one in London could have been regarded as unusual, but in reality there was always some interchange of ships – usually involving a name change and funnel repaint.

Atreus, built 1951, 7,797 tons. Blue Funnel. Royal Albert.
Built by Vickers Armstrong on the Tyne, she was transferred to Elder Dempster Line in 1977, before being sold to become the Liberian *United Valiant*, albeit flying the Singapore flag. She was eventually broken up in Kaohsiung in 1979.

Demodocus, built 1955, 7,964 tons. Blue Funnel. Royal Albert.
Built by Vickers Armstrong. In 1970 she was transferred to the Glen Line as the *Glengarry*, before being returned to Blue Funnel in 1972 and sold to the Chinese in 1973.

Diomed, built 1956, 7,980 tons. Blue Funnel. Royal Albert.
Built by Caledon and transferred to the Glen Line as the *Glenbeg* in 1970. She was returned to Blue
Funnel in 1972 before being sold to Macau/Somali interests in 1973. She was eventually broken up
in 1983.

Hector, built 1950, 10,118 tons. Blue Funnel. Royal Albert.
One of four large passenger/cargo liners built for Blue Funnel. Three of the quartet, of which the
Hector was one, were built by Harland & Wolff. She was broken up at Kaoshiung in 1972.

Royal Miscellany III

General Guisan, built 1957, 6,348 tons. Suisse-Atlantique, Switzerland. Royal Victoria.
The Swiss navy and merchant navy were always the subject of corny and less-than-amusing music hall jokes. Established because of the problems arising from the Second World War, it has celebrated its seventy-fifth anniversary. In the mid-1960s, there were about thirty ships and the total today is over forty. She was the second ship to honour the Second World War general. The first ship, built in West Hartlepool, was the first ship Suisse Atlantique ordered from new. Even today, a large bulk carrier plies the seas, carrying the name and flying the flag.

Lavaux, built 1959, 6,441 tons. Suisse-Atlantique, Switzerland. Royal Albert.
Nothing known, but name is still carried and flag still flying.

Kungaland, built 1951, 7,870 tons. Tirfing Steamship, Sweden. Royal Albert.
Built in Gothenburg, she was sold in 1966, not long after this photograph was taken. She also did not make it into the 1967 edition of *Ocean Ships*. She was eventually scrapped in 1972.

Erkowit, built 1962, Sudan Line, Sudan. Royal Albert.
Another example of the effect of the wind of change.

Harambee, built 1953, 6,169 tons. East African National Shipping Line, Kenya. Royal Albert.
Not one of the best photographs, but a 'must have' because of the unusual flag. Built in the early
1950s at Lubeck and delivered to Hamburg-Sud as the *Belgrano*, she was named *Santa Barbara* in
1965. She was sold in 1966 to East African National Shipping, taking on her third name and flag.
She remained with EAN Shipping until 1979, when she was sold to Panamanian owners and then,
after only one voyage, sold for scrapping in Kaohsiung in 1980. Sadly, the venture to establish a
national shipping company for Kenya, Uganda, Tanzania and Zambia eventually failed and the
company was placed in liquidation in 1980.

Moose Jaw, built 1963. Norway. Royal Victoria.
Built in France as the *Hoegh Beaver* (Hoegh Line), she carried the name *Moose Jaw* from 1964 to
1968 while on a long-term charter to Canadian Pacific, before reverting to her original name. She
was eventually scrapped at Gadani Beach in 1984.

Laganbank, built 1955, 5,671 tons. Bank Line. Royal Albert.
In the early 1950s, Bank Line embarked on a programme of fleet renewal. The strategy was to have fifty general cargo tramp steamers. The *Laganbank* was the last of a batch of six ordered from Harland & Wolff. The choice of name was particularly appropriate.

She was sold to Somali interests in 1973, briefly flying the Cypriot flag before returning to the Somali flag in 1974. She foundered off the coast of West Africa while on a voyage from Bangkok to Apapa (Ghana) in 1978.

Solnechinogorsk, built 1958, 9,518 tons. USSR. Royal Victoria.
One of a number of standard designed cargo ships built for the Communist Bloc. She was one of twenty-nine built in Gdansk, Poland, nine of which were allocated to the Soviet Union. She is seen at the grain elevators in the Royal Victoria Docks. Following the break-up of the Soviet Union, she ended up flying the Ukrainian flag and was eventually scrapped in 1995.

Eemhaven, built 1963, 8,314 tons. Gedr. Van Uden SAM, Netherlands. Royal Albert.
Built at Alblasserdam in the Netherlands and sold in 1983 to Panama, before being sold again for breaking up at Chittagong in 1984.

Prins Maurits, built 1961, 3,995 tons. Oranje Line, Netherlands. Royal Albert.
The Oranje Line, along with the Norwegian Olsen & Ugelstad (Fjell Line), were pioneer operators of a service from Europe to the Great Lakes in the days before the St Lawrence Seaway. *Prins Maurits* was built at Kiel in Germany and sold in 1969, initially to Greece, but after flying several different flags she was eventually scrapped at Alang in 1988.

Prins Willem van Oranje, built 1953, 5,419 tons. Oranje Line, Netherlands. Royal Albert.
Built in the Netherlands and sold in 1965 to East Germany to become the *Ferdinand Freiligrath* and
on to Cyprus in 1974, she was eventually scrapped in Kaohsiung in 1979.

United States Lines

American Traveler, built 1946, 8,228 tons. US Lines. Royal Albert.
Another rare action shot. A modified version of the standard class C2 freighter, she was one of ten
class C2-S-AJ5 freighters built by the North Carolina Shipbuilding Corporation. She was sold to
Amercargo Shipping in 1969 and scrapped in 1972.

American Commander, built 1963, 11,185 tons. US Lines. Royal Victoria.
In the early 1960s, US Lines introduced a new generation of fast (21 knots) cargo vessels called the Challenger class. The pioneer ship in the class, the *American Challenger*, actually achieved a record 24.42 knots on her maiden eastbound voyage. Sadly, their time in commercial service was short lived. The *Commander* was more fortunate. After service in Vietnam, she was retained in the Ready Reserve Fleet and recorded still extant in 2008.

American Crusader, built 1963, 11,244 tons. US Lines. Royal Victoria.
Another example of the Challenger class, disposed of as early as 1967.

Royal Miscellany IV

Custodian, built 1961, 8,847 tons. Harrison Line. Royal Albert.
The Liverpool-based Harrison Line owed its origins to the importing of brandy from the Charente region of France. Named for trades and professions, the *Custodian* was sold to Cyprus in 1979.
 Film buffs and lovers of the writings of Sir Compton MacKenzie will readily recognise that it was a Harrison Liner that was involved in Scotland's most famous wartime shipwreck.

S. A. Hexrivier, built 1966, 6,898 tons. Safmarine, South Africa. Royal Albert.
Refrigerated motor ship built by Verolme in the Netherlands to ship fruit from South Africa to Europe. She was sold in 1977 and, after several changes of ownership and name, was broken up at Alang, Gujarat State, India, in 1994.

S. A. Constantia, built 1968, 12,238 tons. Safmarine. King George V Dock.

While Safmarine is a very successful post-Second World War venture, the sense of tradition still pervades. This ship bears the name of one of the first Victory ships acquired by the newly formed corporation in 1947. Since she entered service in my graduation year, she was virtually brand new and may well be one of the last photographs I took in the London Docks.

Built in Japan, she was one of the last traditional dry cargo ships built for Safmarine. She and her sisters were regarded as having some of the most pleasing lines of the entire fleet. She was eventually disposed of in 1985.

Now part of the Danish Maersk Group, Safmarine still trades as such and ships with the familiar grey hull and containers can still be seen.

Dintledyk, built 1957, 11,366 tons. NASM, Netherlands. Royal Albert.

Established in 1873, NASM, or Holland America Line, was and still is the Dutch equivalent of Cunard. Like Cunard, their passenger liners are now largely employed on cruises. The *Dintledyk* was built by Wilton-Fijenoord in the Netherlands; she operated on a joint service with the UK Royal Mail Line to the North Pacific Coast via the Panama Canal. She was sold in 1970 to C. Y. Tung's Orient Overseas Line to become the *Oriental Fantasia* and eventually scrapped at Kaohsiung in 1978. She was the only cargo liner in the NASM fleet with a grey hull.

Moerdyk, built 1965, 11,127 tons. NASM. Royal Victoria.
This was never the easiest of places to take photographs. The *Moerdyk* was built for Holland America Line (NASM) by Rotterdam Dockyard. She was the fifth of five sisters, described as fast freighters specially adapted to serve the Pacific coast. She was virtually brand new when this picture was taken.

    She was sold to Portugal in 1973 and on to Maltese interests in the spring of 1986. She met her end off the Chinese coast later that year.

Neptune Amber (ex-*Scotia*), built 1966, 5,850 tons. Singapore. King George V Dock.
It has often been noted that a British ship is sold on for further trading to an operator who sails under a different flag. This is the after effect. Originally built as the *Scotia* by Cammell Laird and specially equipped with an ice-breaking bow for the Great Lakes service, she was actually owned by United Dominions Leasing and chartered to Cunard. She became the Singapore-flagged *Neptune Amber* in 1970 and, after being further sold to Indian buyers in 1977, was broken up in Mumbai in 1984.

Przyiazn Narodow (ex-*Marchen Maersk*), built 1937, 8,876 tons. Polish Ocean Lines, Poland. Royal Albert.

Not the best of photographs, partly because of the shortcomings of not using or possessing a single lens reflex camera. However, the ship is particularly interesting. In the inter-war period, a number of Dutch and Danish ships were built with maierform bows. Built in Germany by Bremer Vulkan for A. P. Moller's Maersk Line as the *Marchen Maersk*, she was initially capable of 16 knots. Taken over by the US Navy as a troop transport during the Second World War and named *Perida*, she was returned to her Danish owners and reverted to her original name in 1946. She was acquired by Polish Ocean Lines in 1951 and eventually demolished at Whampoa in 1972.

I was reliably informed by a Polish work colleague that the name meant 'friendship or perhaps fellowship of nations'.

Tilbury Docks

Tilbury is on the north (Essex) shore of the Thames, 25 miles downstream of London Bridge. The Thames meanders south at this point, leaving a large area of marshland. The river also narrows to a width of 800 yards. The London & St Katharine Dock Co., having opened in 1880 their Royal Albert dock with its access at Gallions Reach (11 miles downstream of London Bridge), forced the rival East & West India Docks Co. to retaliate. An Act of Parliament in 1882 enabled the company to retaliate and work started in earnest to build the new docks within a fortnight of the Act being passed. They were opened four years later in 1886.

The docks were absorbed into the Port of London Authority in 1909. Considerable improvements were undertaken in 1921 and 1929, with further extensions in the 1960s. The new £30-million container port opened in 1967, but protracted labour disputes delayed full operation until 1970. By 1980, closures upstream led to Tilbury becoming the only enclosed docks operated by the PLA. A further deepwater container terminal was added in 1978.

Beira, built 1963, 8,701 tons. Cia Nacional de Navegacao Portuguese, Portugal. Tilbury.
When completed in the Netherlands, she was the largest ship in the very small Portuguese merchant navy. She was sold in 1983 and scrapped in Bombay.

Ulcinj (ex-*Martin Zubizarreta*), built 1961, 8,215 tons. Prekoskeanska Plovidba Bar, Yugoslavia.
Originally built in Bilbao, Spain, for Spanish owners, this photograph was taken in 1969, shortly after the change of ownership and name had taken place. The funnel colours indicate the state-owned *Jugolinja* (Yugoslav Line).

Robert Stove, built 1963, 20,463 tons. Norway Tilbury.
A large freighter/bulk carrier caught on a very wet afternoon at Tilbury. The deluge predicted when I photographed the *Indian Tradition* had arrived! She became the *Somali Andaman Sea* in 1973, before passing through several Chinese owners until 1999.

Palm Line

Palm Line was formed from the United Africa Company in 1949. The company traded along the African coast from Morocco to Angola. To navigate the many creeks, the ships had to be less than 500 feet long and draw not more than 27 feet. To enter the Escravos river in Nigeria, a maximum of 17 feet was permitted over the bar.

The 1980s saw the end of Palm Line. A decline in traffic between Europe and West Africa resulted in the company being sold in 1986.

Africa Palm, built 1953, 5,410 tons. Palm Line. Tilbury.
Built by Short Bros. in Sunderland and sold in 1972 to Gulf Shipping to become the *Savoydean*, flying the Panamanian flag. In July 1975 she caught fire in Calcutta while en route from Chittagong to Africa with a cargo of jute and hessian. Declared a constructive total loss, she was broken up at Bombay in April 1976.

Andoni Palm, built 1958, 5,802 tons. Palm Line. Tilbury.
Built in Germany by Bremer Vulkan. She was sold to Panama in 1976 and scrapped in 1982.

Burutu Palm, built 1952, 5,410 tons. Palm Line. Tilbury.
Built by Shorts, Sunderland. Sold to Greece to become the *Thyi* in 1967, just after I bought my
second Moody *Ocean Ships*. In 1973 she was sold onto Singapore to become the *Globe Star*, but
ran aground on the notorious Leven reef off Mombasa the same year. Attempts to refloat her failed,
and heavy seas caused the ship to break up. Largely demolished in 1975, the wreck remains a
popular diving spot.

Elder Dempster Line

Elder Dempster was originally founded in 1868 to trade from Glasgow and Liverpool to West Africa. In 1909 control passed to Sir Owen Philips. After the collapse of the Royal Mail group, the company came under the management control of Blue Funnel. In 1957, when Nigerian National Line was established, the company took a 33 per cent share, selling out to the Nigerian government in 1961. In 1965 the company came under complete control of Blue Funnel.

The shipping company ceased when sold out to the French Delmas-Vieljeux. The shipping agency was wound up in 2000.

Ebani, built 1952, 9,397 tons. Elder Dempster. Tilbury.
Built by Scotts of Greenock, originally for the North America–West Africa service. Later she was deployed on the UK–West Africa run and briefly operated by Blue Funnel on the Far East service in 1973. She was scrapped in 1977.

Egori, built 1957, 8,586 tons. Elder Dempster. Tilbury.
Built by Scotts of Greenock and sold to Kuwait to become the *Azza* in 1978.

Falaba, built 1962, 7,703 tons. Elder Dempster. Tilbury.
Built by Scotts of Greenock, she was the second of six 'F' class ships, which proved to be the last traditional freighters built for Elder Dempster. She traded for Mexican owners from 1978 before she was sold to Greece in 1980 and broken up in Chittagong in October 1984.

Tilbury Miscellany

Capetan Manolis, built 1969, A. Alafouzos, Greece. Tilbury.
This is an SD14. The SD14 was a 1960s project to replace the many aging Liberty and Victory ships with a cheap, modern standard tramp steamer. The first orders came from Greece. One of the first, the *Capetan Manolis* was built by Bartrams of Sunderland; she was eventually sold to India in 1978. Laid up in Bombay in 1985, she was sent for scrapping in 1988 but, for some bizarre and inexplicable reason, she was not finally scrapped until 2003!

Fritz Heckert, built 1961, 8,115 tons. East Germany. Tilbury.
My only photograph of a passenger ship at Tilbury. A small cruise ship built to carry or reward 379 passengers or successful workers. Decommissioned in 1970, she was used as an accommodation ship until 1991, when she was sold to become a hotel ship in Dubai. She was eventually scrapped in Mumbai in 1999.

Cerdic Ferry, built 1961, 3,333 tons. Atlantic S N. Tilbury.
Even in the mid-1960s, tucked away at Tilbury was a ro-ro service to mainland Europe. The *Cerdic Ferry* was built by Ailsa Shipbuilding. She was sold to Greece in 1989 and, after various changes of ownership, was eventually scrapped in Aliaga in 2007. The ro-ro service, now a much larger and busier operation between Tilbury and Zeebrugge, continues today with some ships clearly displaying the P&O house flag, if not the red ensign.

Rio Mar, built pre-1967, 16,334 tons. Liberia. Tilbury.
Described on the web as a bulker built between 1961 and 1970. This was the summer of 1966. She was broken up in Greece in 1984.

Indian Tradition, built 1960, 7,150 tons. Indian Steamship, India. Tilbury.
Indian Steamship was founded in 1929 and traded a liner service between the subcontinent and Europe. *Indian Tradition* was built in Hamburg and broken up in Bombay in 1980. I always thought this was one of my best photographs, with the background of heavy clouds indicating an imminent deluge.

American Astronaut, built 1968, 18,876 tons. US Lines. Tilbury.
The first batch of US Lines container ships were designated C7 Lancer and all had 'L' names. The mood of the times, with space exploration and moon landings, prompted the choice of name. Following the bankruptcy of US Lines, the ships were sold and she became the *Guayuna* and was eventually scrapped in 2002.

The picture shows interesting contrasts. The new container gantries are alongside traditional cranes.

Encounter Bay, built 1969, 26,756 tons. OCL. Tilbury.

Overseas Container Lines was formed as a joint venture consortium of British & Commonwealth (Clan Line and Union-Castle), Furness Withy, P&O and Blue Funnel. Over the years, P&O gradually took control, finally gaining complete control in 1987 with the company becoming P&O Containers. In 1996 it merged with Nedlloyd to form P&O Nedlloyd, which again became part of the Maersk Group in 2005.

The *Encounter Bay* was the pioneer. Substantially larger (still midgets by today's standards) than the American C7 Lancer class, she was built in Hamburg, Germany, and made her maiden voyage from Rotterdam to Australia in March 1969. Both events clearly indicate the state and image of both British shipbuilding and labour relations in the port industry at the time. She remained with the fleet until scrapped in Panyu China in 1999.

The choice of 'Bay' names recalled the old Australian Commonwealth Line, taken over by the Kylsant Group in 1928. When the Kylsant Group collapsed in 1933 the ships were transferred to the Shaw Savill Line under the title Aberdeen & Commonwealth Line. The Bay names remained until the final Maersk takeover, and even then, no names were changed.

LONDON DOCKS
IN THE 1960S